The W... Spinoza and Gurdjieff

LEWIS ALMEIDA

Copyright © 2022 Lewis Almeida.
All rights reserved.

Almeida Publications
Santa Monica, California

WayofSpinoza.com

About the case studies in this book:
I have changed the names of my
students out of respect for their privacy.

Cover and interior design by Philip Wyeth.
www.philipwyeth.com

CONTENTS

Introduction	i
Knowing Oneself	1
Betty Case Study	2
Fear of Confrontation	6
Lying to Ourselves	9
The Process of Strengthening the Mind	10
The Voice of the Ego	10
Man is Asleep	11
Emotion of Desire	13
The Being of Man	15
Freedom from Emotions	16
Nature's Laws	18
Jesus the Man	20
The Essence of Man	22
Improvement of the Understanding	25
God's Attributes	27
The Nature of the Work	29
Spinoza's Language	29
A Poem: "Mysterious Path" by Frederick Kettner	32
My Thoughts	32
Gregory Grover Teacher	33
Attracting New Students	34
Essay: "Being a Student"	35
Comments	36

Carol Case Study	37
Carol Factualizing	40
Louis C.K.	43
Carol Embracing Spinoza	44
Ted's Poem to His Mom	45
Factualizing and Journaling	46
Definition of Pain	47
Being in Touch with Our Pain	48
Problems of Addiction	49
Perfection and Reality	51
Importance of a Teacher	54
Resistance to Change	54
The Process of Transformation	55
Emailing with David	59
Overview of David's Interest	64
Gurdjieff "Personality and Essence"	66
Belief in Free Will	68
Gurdjieff "Magnetic Center"	69
The Mind	72
As Children	73
Free Will	74
Case Study: Laura Next Door	76
Mind and Body Connection	81
When the Body Says No	82
My Comments on the Book	83
Medical Field Lacks Understanding	84
Emotional Disconnection Causes Cancer	85

The Unconscious Parent	86
Spinoza's *Ethics*	88
Spinoza's God	89
Knowledge and Being	91
My Comments on Gurdjieff and Being	91
Poem: "Wait with Rejoicing"	93
My Comments on the Poem	93
Intuition is Necessary	94
Spinoza on the Bible	95
Spinoza on Jesus and Moses	96
Spinoza: A New Character	97
Improvement of Our Understanding	100
Regarding Gurdjieff	101
On Reason	102
My Comments on Reason and Desire	102
Man's Inhumanity	105
The Conscious Parent	107
Being a Teacher	107
Teacher's Essay: "Solving Life's Problems"	109
My Comments on the Essay	110
A Lazy Mind	111
Understanding the *Ethics*	112
Understanding Spinoza	115
The Awakening Process	119
An Active State	121
Ego and Personality	121

Spinoza on Perfection	123
Improving Our Understanding	124
Boy on a Skateboard	126
Spinoza's Method	127
My Own Growth	130
The Emotions	131
Dolores Case Study	134
Spinoza on Active and Passive Mind	135
God and the Mind	136
Desire is the Essence of Man	137
Meaningful Relationships	138
Letter to Students	141
Letter of Gratitude	144
Comments on Aaron's Letter	145
Attraction to the Work	146
A Former Student	149
Developing the Understanding	153
Gregory Grover	155
Susan Compares Buddhism to Spinoza	156
Easter Sunday	158
The Spirit of Jesus	159
Jesus and Barabbas	161
Jack Case Study	163
Movie *Ordinary People*	166
Steve's Email	169
Personal Story	176

Essay: "Discriminating Between Your Intelligence and Memory"	177
My Comments on Memory and Intelligence	178
Hugh Case Study	180
Paul Case Study	182
Matt Case Study	183
Idea of Effort	184
Ben Case Study	185
Jennifer Case Study	186
A Final Note	188

INTRODUCTION

Many books have been written about Baruch Spinoza's philosophy. University professors often find themselves overwhelmed as they hurriedly grasp bits and pieces from the various Spinoza texts. But collecting random fragments is no way to go about understanding the core teachings of such an important thinker – and thus their students also suffer.

While studying under the late Gregory Grover for many years, I internalized the complex ideas that characterize Spinoza's language. His towering philosophy teaches us the possibility of coming to a new character. His *Ethics* – when digested, assimilated, and embraced – can be understood when we dedicate our entire being: mentally, emotionally, and physically.

Freedom from emotional bondage is possible when we learn to apply our understanding. It is through examining our emotions that we begin to strengthen the mind's understanding. Eventually, as our mental strength increases, it is also possible to understand the laws and nature of God non-anthropomorphically.

Spinoza's ideas should be approached not as mere written words, but as a living reality which offers us the tools of reason and intuition. With Spinoza's philosophy communicated by the right teacher as a guide, our lives can be changed for the better.

A new character is born, a character that is free from the negative emotions of fear, hate, and anger. A knowledge that we are part of the wholeness of Nature or God.

In this work of improving our understanding, we develop our own authority to gain a sense of self and self-approval. When we are less concerned about the opinions of others, it is also possible to become a master of one's emotions.

Desire to understand and loving our efforts in wanting to improve the clarity of our thinking is possible. The mind knows and tastes its clarity and its connection with the Divine. Therefore, true happiness is knowing oneself through reason and intuition and having a direct commune with Her Divinity.

This book examines real case studies to give insights into the process of learning, understanding, and awakening the mind. It is for the individual who aspires to something beyond the ordinary, who seeks happiness, a purpose, and a meaningful life.

Now, let us begin the journey together as students of Spinoza's great works…

-Lewis Almeida
Santa Monica, CA
January 2022

Knowing Oneself

Over two thousand years ago, Socrates proclaimed, "To know oneself is the highest level of knowledge." Likewise, Spinoza's *Ethics* expresses the importance of awakening our intelligence. The process of acknowledging and understanding our emotions by using the tools of reason and intuition can lead us to freedom, peace, and fulfillment.

However, to understand Spinoza's philosophy, an emotion of genuine desire to understand and the love of our efforts is necessary. We must learn how to apply his knowledge to improve our nature that is resistant to change. Applying Spinoza's methods with an open heart and pure intention has the potential to transform your life.

The goal and purpose of Spinoza's work was to comprehend the union that exists between the human mind and the whole of nature. My role as teacher is to guide seekers through this process of coming to see and understand that great union, and in turn connect with the wholeness of Nature.

An important part of grasping this knowledge begins by examining our nature. We must ask, how are we affected emotionally by the daily challenges and events that trigger us? It is in this examination; we begin to learn how to see our nature without judgments. Our emotions tell a story about how we see life's challenges and disappointments. This process is learning how to see objectively with an open mind.

The question often arises: "Why does God allow suffering? Why is there so much suffering in the world?"

Spinoza explains that once we understand the nature of suffering itself, our own suffering ceases.

Consider this sequence: Suffering is pain. It is a feeling of powerlessness, helplessness, emptiness, and not knowing what to do. This painful condition is a weak state of being which causes an inability to act decisively or face one's problems. When life's challenges demand more from us than we can give, we may brood angrily, run away, or simply procrastinate.

Man can only free himself after he understands the true nature of his pain and suffering. This is achieved through the process of strengthening his intelligence.

The following case study is an example of how to work through our pain and confusion to gain understanding as well as more control over our lives.

Betty Case Study

Betty came to me wanting to know more about Spinoza; thinking that his ideas were clear and promising. Betty wanted to come to a deeper sense of self with more clarity and truth.

I explained that to begin to understand Spinoza's language, we must start with where we are. In reality, we are egocentric; meaning that we live in an ego state. This is our identity; we have a personality that expresses the ego. The ego uses the memory for its knowledge. The knowledge that we acquired since infancy.

George Gurdjieff, an early twentieth century Russian philosopher and mystic, explains that man is asleep and the goal is to awaken the greater part of our mind that is seldom used.

Our true intelligence operates in the reality of the now. The daily problems we face are opportunities for us to grow as our intelligence improves and strengthens its understanding. The goal and purpose are to live from this intelligence in an enlightened state of being. However, it takes time, patience, and dissatisfaction with where you are, and the desire for something that will give a deeper meaning and purpose.

Betty's problem was she did not understand why she was so angry. On one occasion, while she and her boyfriend Rick were at a restaurant, Betty saw that he was flirting with other women while they were having dinner.

She felt pain, hate, and anger. I suggested that she keep a journal and write about what drew her to be involved with Rick. Because first, she needed to acknowledge and articulate her desire – what was it that she wanted?

Betty revealed that she wanted to be loved and appreciated. I suggested that she accept she was in pain, to be with it and surrender to the feeling rather than run from it.

Facing our emotions in this direct way can trigger and awaken our true intelligence. This intelligence is different from our normal ego-intellect which addresses commonplace situations while we go about our daily lives.

This intelligence, when awakened, wants to improve its understanding through truth and clarity. It is the active part of the mind that wants to understand, and it is in the understanding that we gain a new sense of self through the power of clarity.

There are two aspects to the mind, active and passive. The active part expresses clear ideas and endeavors to understand. The passive part is comprised of confused and fragmentary information; it depends on memory and an unconscious automatic response state.

Your background and the environment you grew up in automatically conditioned you to accept so many things about the world without ever questioning them. The memory contains set patterns of how to behave and handle problems. If our childhood was spent in a fearful environment, it's logical that we would constantly be worried, envious, have feelings of inferiority, and always compare ourselves to others.

And yet, despite this lingering childhood trauma, we still believe we have free will and dictate our own desires, actions, and reactions.

When Betty believes that Rick is the cause of her pain, she begins to hate him. Hate is pain directed at an external cause. What follows hate is anger. Anger is the manifestation of hatred which induces us to remove or destroy the perceived source of our pain.

Are you beginning to see why I say that no one willfully feels hate or anger?

I suggested to Betty that she put in the effort to journal her experiences, even if she didn't quite understand why she was being asked to do so. This is the role of the teacher – to safely guide the student, who in turn must have faith and trust in the purpose of their assignments.

The work is difficult because it often requires us to understand a new language, the knowledge expressed in Spinoza and Gurdjieff's teachings and philosophy.

This wisdom will come to you over time with effort – it will become a part of you. All you have to do is make the commitment. As we get more comfortable living within the reality of increased active intelligence, we can examine our true nature honestly and without defensive reactions.

The goal is to see how the ego-self is really in a sleep state of being, and relies upon memory while operating like a programmed machine.

No one has demonstrated to you that you have an intelligence that is different from the passive ego-intellect. We all are born into an environment that only wants to know how to function and exist in society; however, it is a passive sleep state, a semiconscious state of being and depends solely on memory.

This ego state basically lives through the reality constructed by our cumulative memory stored in the brain. Only our awakened intelligence can break out of the pattern by actively seeking knowledge and striving to understand it.

This clarity enables us to assess when we are feeling confident and accept when we are confused. This is a powerful balance between power and humility.

Fear of Confrontation

Ken has been working with me as a student for eight months. He is a highly intellectual type, loves philosophy, and spends a lot of his time reading scientific material. He fears emotional confrontation and is unable to say no to other people. Instead he turns off his phone and will not answer emails. Although he is successful as a corporate attorney, he wants to change careers because it is too stressful.

Ken brought up a situation he wanted to study. He was having lunch with an old friend named Charles and told him that he was planning to attend a mutual friend's wedding. It turns out that Charles wasn't invited, but he wanted to go because he had nothing to do, was lonely, wanted to meet women, and get a free dinner.

Ken did not know what to say. He felt pressured to say yes, but was also in fear that the groom would disapprove. Ken felt stress, pain, discomfort, and didn't know what to do. While he wanted to say no, he could only reply with, "That is an odd request."

Ken could not be direct and simply say no to Charles. He did not want to cause his friend pain and was afraid of any emotional unknowns. Ken fears emotional confrontation, so he just avoids the issue and hopes that it will go away.

For Ken to improve and come to a higher level of being and change his character, he must force himself to get in touch with his emotions and feelings. This will take time, effort, patience, and trusting me as his teacher to walk him through the process of factualizing the events that stress him out and making the effort to be in touch with his feelings and emotions.

Ken is now seeing the problem and feels encouraged. He wants to change and not live in fear. We all must want something more and be dissatisfied with where we are in order to improve.

Remember, we have no choice or free will, we follow from the law of necessity. The law of necessity means that we will do whatever we believe will handle the issues and problems we face, according to the knowledge we have learned since infancy. A pattern of behavior is developed necessarily to help preserve our existence. Therefore, it is necessary that we do what we do to preserve our existence.

Again, I say that pain is a feeling of powerlessness, helplessness, impotence, and not knowing what to do. It starts when we feel that our desires are not being fulfilled, and we aren't getting what we want out of life.

When we blame others for causing our pain, we begin to hate them and want to punish them. Hate is an emotion. Hate is pain accompanied by the idea of an external cause. The key is to understand your emotions and eventually learn how to observe without judgments. Acknowledge your pain, surrender to it, and go deeper.

What is this feeling? You feel powerless, helpless, empty, and really do not know what to do.

As you go through this process, staying in the moment and surrendering to the feelings, something miraculous happens!

Our true intelligence will awaken because it is the nature of the mind to desire to understand. This is distinct from our ego-intellect, which constantly compares, lives in fear, wants to feel superior, constantly seeks approval from others, and fears rejection.

Spinoza's idea that we follow the law of necessity and self-preservation, rather than act upon a sense of free will, is a confusing concept. It's such a radical idea that many people reject Spinoza altogether.

Their first response is to say, "What do you mean I have no choices in life? That is ridiculous!"

Spinoza explains this complex issue by saying that while we are aware of our immediate desires and actions, we remain ignorant of their causes and how they determine our nature by directing us to behave in certain ways when desire affects us.

In Spinoza's *Ethics*, particularly "On the Improvement of the Understanding," he presents a method to awaken the higher mind that is our innate intelligence which expresses the understanding. By improving our understanding, we learn how our nature works and why we are affected by life's influences, and how we are capable of increasing our mental powers to think clearly.

Most of us exist in a semi-conscious, sleep-state of being – however, it is possible to awaken.

Lying to Ourselves

Gurdjieff explains that it easy to lie to ourselves and imagine that we are making progress, when in reality we're only rearranging the imaginary furniture in our mental world. We choose to go it alone because many of us have never felt that someone else was really listening to us. That frustration causes us to fear opening up to expose our shortcomings and feelings of inadequacy.

Therefore, finding the right teacher we can trust is so important while guiding us along the healing process of examining our nature.

Gurdjieff explains that our being expresses many desires, attitudes, beliefs, habits, and patterns of thinking. Our being at times expresses courage, fear, love, hate, compassion, giving, truthfulness, deceitfulness, lying, etc.

Gurdjieff explains this on pp. 161-164 of P.D. Ouspensky's book *In Search of the Miraculous*. He says, "There is a great difference between essence and personality. Essence is that which is our own, personality is that which is not our own."

Our own means that we affirm the power of our thinking and the effort to understand, and what we understand cannot be taken from us. It is truly our own. Personality is all of the information that we have learned since infancy – our programmed conditioned nature – and which is followed blindly without any understanding as to why we do what we do.

The Process of Strengthening the Mind

Journaling our experiences that trigger us activates the mind, because it loves to work on problems and the confusing aspects of our lives. It gains strength as it endeavors to understand the problems that feel overwhelming.

The ego-intellect is the passive part of the mind that relies on memory, is constantly comparing itself to others, lives in fear, and believes in free will. It is important for us to know the difference between the true intelligence and our ego-memory mind. When we increase our efforts to understand this distinction, we gain a deeper and stronger sense of self.

Our voice represents the active thinking mind that understands the law of necessity and the law of self-preservation. Active thinking is primary and comes about as we enjoy our efforts to understand, and a successful result is secondary.

The Voice of the Ego

When the voice of the ego is dominant, it seeks pride for its accomplishments. Why? Because the ego believes in free will. It says, "I did this!"

Pride causes us to bask in the glow of our deeds. But lingering in the past, no matter how successful, inhibits the flow of creativity. We ignore the present reality around us and lose connection to the true intelligence of our active mind.

The ego expresses a passive part of our nature because it relies on memory. It reflects a false sense of self: it is only an image, the ghost of who we really are.

All emotions manifest from the illusion that we have free will. We are led astray by the belief that we are the direct cause of our desires and actions. We remain unaware of the root causes of our desires and how they direct and determine our lives.

The ego desires excessive power over others. It is prideful, envious, and contemptuous. It inhabits the lowest level of knowledge, operating through hearsay and unconscious experience. It is oblivious to the broader outside reality, of natural causes and effects, and how the world influences and directs our whole being.

Man is Asleep

Gurdjieff explains that because man is asleep, it is impossible for him to understand the laws of nature, the law of necessity, and the law of self-preservation.

As my student Larry examined his feelings of hate, he began to understand the definition of hate itself. Because hate is pain attributed to an external cause, he automatically believed the cause of his pain was his unfaithful wife.

This hate then turned to anger. Anger is desire, whereby through hatred we are induced to remove, destroy, or run away from the object of our hate.

Are you beginning to see a pattern here? This pattern will repeat itself over and over again.

It begins with desire. We want something or expect something, and if our desire is not met, then we feel pain. We move from pain to hate, and from hate to anger. This is the destructive cycle which has cursed mankind throughout its entire existence.

This process is automatic because our minds exist in a passive state. Even when we feel our blood boil, in truth we are behaving like programmed robots without consciousness.

And yet, the higher level of intelligence exists within all of us. It is innate, waiting to be awakened from a dormant state to unleash its great potential.

As Spinoza explains in proposition 1, part 3 of the *Ethics*, "That in certain cases the mind is active, and in certain cases the mind is passive." Being active means that the mind is comprised of clear and distinct ideas, it endeavors to understand, and this understanding will become our new identity.

It truly is a source of freedom and oneness to aspire to connect with Spinoza's God, the infinite and eternal being expressed by Nature.

Emotion of Desire

We are aware or semi-conscious of our desires and our emotional reactions, but unconscious of how they determine our existence. We are born with the idea of free will and never question it.

Spinoza explains that there are three levels of knowledge.

1. Hearsay and experience, superficial knowledge.

2. Reason, being able to see how things are connected, rational thinking.

3. Intuition, knowing directly, the reality of nature, and understanding the causes and effects of things, and how all things are connected with the whole of nature.

Hearsay and experience represent the lowest level of knowledge. As children, we trust our authority figures and follow them dogmatically. We are conditioned to behave in a certain way by mimicking others – these learned behaviors and attitudes feed our imagination. Consequently, we have no independent sense of "I," no real power that we can call our own. All of our knowledge is borrowed, copied, and imitated since childhood.

This is the root cause of our suffering!

Our inner being was never nourished, therefore it is impossible to feel worthy, self-love, or have any sense of self-acceptance. We forever seek pleasure and avoid pain on a primal level as we act upon the law of necessity and the law of self-preservation. However, we still believe we are free because the notion has been handed down through the ages.

Spinoza, in his studies of Plato, Socrates, the Stoics, and especially Descartes, examined man's nature more deeply. His intuition took him beyond the work of these other philosophers into new frontiers of thought as he began to conceive of a whole new reality.

He employed reason and intuition to demonstrate his mental clarity and this higher truth. He even applied Euclid's geometric methodology in his *Ethics* to demonstrate his ideas mathematically.

Spinoza explained the relationship between the mind and the body; how the body is affected and modified by external objects; and how the mind is also simultaneously affected by such changes in the body. In other words, the mind and body work as one, but at the same time expressing two distinct attributes of God's nature: the attribute of thought and the attribute of extension.

Through understanding our emotions it is possible to free ourselves from them. Descartes and the Stoics believed that the human mind had power to control our emotions by willpower alone. Spinoza disagreed and went on to prove that this idea had no merit or truth.

Why does man believe in free will, and that his choices are made freely? Why does he believe that he chooses his own emotions and desires?

This blind hubris demonstrates that man is not aware of how limited his consciousness really is. He is in a semi-conscious state at best!

Gurdjieff calls this a sleep state and gives us an insight into the nature of man.

On pages 65-66 of *In Search of the Miraculous*, Gurdjieff's student Ouspensky explains that there is a great difference between knowledge and being. The being of man is his essence – that is, the idea and the nature of man. Who he is, all his thoughts, confusions, beliefs, habits, and patterns of behavior – everything about him which aids in the effort to exist and persist.

He may have the practical knowledge that comes with being a doctor, attorney, engineer, or plumber, and being very successful in life. Yet his core being has not changed at all despite his profession, popularity, or wealth.

He might still be a mean, sarcastic, narcissistic, abusive, and contemptuous person. Therefore, intellectual knowledge alone is insufficient to help us develop a higher level of consciousness or improve our nature.

The Being of Man

What is the being of man's nature?

The being of the individual is everything that represents and expresses his character and nature. This includes his beliefs, attitudes, confusions, and sense of clarity. His being may express itself through happiness, sadness, anger, hate, love, compassion, etc.

Gurdjieff explains that all of this information is a man's knowledge about how to preserve his existence. It is stored in his memory and relied upon to automatically handle challenging problems. If we do not have the proper information or the intelligent resources to handle difficulties, we often react automatically like robotic machines and lose control of our emotions.

This is because man cannot see beyond his conditioned nature. It is as if he is blind to the true reality of his inner existence.

Gurdjieff calls this buffering. Buffering is like having blinders on that prevent us from seeing the truth. However, buffers also serve as a form of self-protection when we are not willing to face how confused we really are. In turn, they protect us when we are not capable of looking at our weaknesses or confusions.

The process of buffering and ignoring reality is an inborn part of man's nature. He imagines and pretends that all is well within, and believes that he has free will to choose to ignore the problems that plague his life. He simply does not want to be disturbed or awakened to this reality.

Freedom from Emotions

The mind consists of two parts: active and passive. As Spinoza explains in proposition 1, part 3 of the *Ethics*, "In certain cases the mind is active, and in certain cases the mind is passive."

The passive part of the mind relies on memory – this is where all information acquired since infancy is stored in our brain.

This is also where the ego is formed. The ego is an identity that developed automatically, and its acts as the shadow of the self.

The active part of the mind is the awakened part. It endeavors to think clearly and adequately by applying effort to understand through reason and intuition.

Freedom from emotions must come from our intelligence and by using the active part of the mind.

Every student must go through a deliberate process to awaken their intelligence. The process is both challenging and rewarding, and makes it possible for you to develop a whole new sense of self: an awakened intelligence that lives in the reality of the now.

However, in order to succeed we must first learn to see ourselves without judgments or false narratives.

Thus unencumbered, we soon begin to realize that we are not really aware of our actual nature. In fact, we are only semi-conscious and exist in a sleep state of being.

Only the truly awakened intelligence thinks with the Mind of God and is connected with the source.

"What is this source?" you might ask. "What is God?"

The source is the Infinite Being… or Nature… It is Spinoza's God. (I must stress, however, that this is a non-anthropomorphic Being. It is not a personal God.)

One reason that I include Gurdjieff in my work is because he complements Spinoza to a great degree. Gurdjieff is a crucial stepping stone in introducing you to the reality that man is asleep and must awaken.

Gurdjieff also points out that man will deliberately, although not necessarily out of free will, prevent any opportunity for such a personal awakening. His innate being prevents it!

Man often remains complacent or stagnant, no matter how painful his current state of being might be. Why? Because he is reluctant to leave what is familiar.

Nature's Laws

Man lives by the laws of his nature. He will do anything to maintain his existence while putting forth the least amount of effort possible. Man also lives by his emotions. Consequently, the higher levels of consciousness and intuition are not available to him during normal life.

There must be a dissatisfaction with his life, a crisis point where he grasps an intuitive feeling that there's more out there for him, even if he can't see what it actually is.

The good news is that when a prospective student is ready, the teacher appears. And when that teacher is found, the student must want to do the work desperately and genuinely. He must believe that the work will help free him from painful emotions, and that with total commitment happiness and fulfillment are possible.

We can read philosophical books, listen to podcasts, and attend very expensive seminars promising that you'll achieve a higher level of consciousness just for showing up. However, simply listening cannot change your basic beliefs, perspectives, attitudes, and habits. All are too deeply rooted and entrenched in your being to be conquered by willpower alone.

This is why Spinoza is so important – he developed a method of how to awaken the power of our true intelligence after personally going through a process of transformation.

As a young man he wanted what everyone else thinks they want: wealth, fame, and to indulge the pleasures of the senses. But over time, Spinoza began to understand that these desires can become excessive, consuming and overwhelming so that we have no time to think of anything else.

Spinoza was born into the Jewish faith and lived in a Jewish community in Amsterdam during the 17th century. He was formally educated, studied the Torah, and was also influenced by secular philosophers like Socrates, Plato, Hume, and the Stoics, among others. The work of Descartes inspired Spinoza to the greatest extent, and later developed a geometric method to explain and prove his own philosophical ideas.

Here is where I want to emphasize that Spinoza's philosophy is of such a nature that it transcends mere theoretical concepts. It is a comprehensive way of living that includes psychology, philosophy, science, mathematics, and the study of the human body.

Many of today's scholars and university professors only study Spinoza intellectually. While able to explain some of his ideas from an academic perspective, overlooking the emotional connection misses the practical applications that his philosophy offers. Too much theoretical pontificating without the real-world test demonstrates an incomplete understanding of Spinoza's work.

Jesus the Man

I see Jesus as having both wisdom about human nature and knowledge of the Infinite Being's true essence.

Many biographical aspects of His life are actually symbolic or allegorical. A literal-minded person might consider these to be childish stories, and miss out on the deeper meaning. The mind of man is extremely weak and he will believe anything if the false concepts are repeated enough.

Jesus was asked why he communicated with the masses in the form of parables. He answered, "To [my disciples] it has been given to know the secrets of the kingdom of God; but to others I speak in parables, so that 'looking they may not perceive, and listening they may not understand.' "

He means that the masses are ignorant by default. As good as it is that some people are perceptive enough to grasp the true nature of reality – equally good that the blind remain blind.

Jesus says in one parable that you cannot put new wine into old wineskins. Back in biblical times, over two thousand years ago, people used the skin of an animal as a vessel for wine, water, etc. Therefore, if you put fresh wine into a wineskin that had previously been used, it would contaminate and spoil the wine.

What is the idea behind this obscure parable? How can we apply it to modern life?

The lesson is crucial to understand: it is impossible for us to accept new ideas that are contrary to what we already believe. We cannot add new ideas to our mind if it is already filled to the brim with preconceived notions.

One of the major causes of resistance when it comes to embracing and understanding new ideas is that we deeply believe that we have free will. We are convinced that we can get all the things we want by the power of choice. This erroneous and destructive belief is followed by over seven billion people on this planet.

And yet, Spinoza proved back in the 17th century that there are laws expressed by nature which govern and determine man's existence. We are determined by the laws of nature into which we are born – we are not smarter or greater than it.

One such limiting guide is the law of necessity: it is necessary that you act upon the knowledge that you have. Necessity is a very special idea that Spinoza emphasizes in his philosophy.

The law of necessity is that everything follows from the laws of nature. It implies that we do not have free will or free choice. What determines our nature are notions, beliefs, habits, and attitudes. All of this is knowledge about how to preserve and persist in our existence.

What you do and why you do it is necessary, even if you regret it. You are doing the best you can with the knowledge you currently have.

For example, if you react angrily to an upsetting situation, you imagine that you are expressing yourself freely in your desire to remove, destroy, or just walk away from the problem. You do not realize that the true cause is much deeper and stems from your confused perception the overall situation: you are in pain and your desires are not being met. In turn, you feel powerless, helpless, and have no idea what to do.

The root of the problem is that you don't understand how the entirety of your knowledge being comprised of confused ideas guarantees frustration. Consequently, the expressions of anger and hate you automatically manifest are misdirected and bring no resolution or improvement.

The misconception that we have free will must be stated repeatedly because we instinctively resist acknowledging it could even be possible. It will take time to understand the painful truth and realize the magnitude of how this fallacious idea leads us astray each day.

The Essence of Man

Spinoza explains the primal nature of human desire.

"Desire is the actual essence of man. In so far as it is conceived, as determined to a particular activity by some given modification of itself."

Both desire and appetite are one and the same, and are determined to act in a way which tends to promote its own persistence. Meaning, that desire or appetite is wanting something that the individual believes or has been conditioned to believe that the thing that it desires will help persist in his or her existence.

As Spinoza explains, we do not have free will and are influenced and preconditioned by urges that we are unconscious of: our desires determine us to follow what we are familiar with that will help us preserve our existence. In the whole of Nature, there is no right or wrong, good or bad; however, we will do whatsoever we feel and believe will help us persist in our existence. Again, the causes of our desires were determined by other causes, and those by other causes and so on, and so on.

How do I know this? I too as a young man of twenty-five began reading self-help books and later, began attending very expensive seminars. They all sounded great, yet nothing changed for me.

It was not until 1970 when I met my teacher, the late Mr. Gregory Grover, that a path opened up for me. I remained his student for over twenty years, and it has taken me another two decades to strengthen my mind as I endeavor to understand Spinoza's ideas and learn to live from them because I wanted to communicate his clarity and truth in how it can awaken man.

What I am conveying to you is the reality of how to really change the direction of your life. If you are bogged down with negative emotions from childhood trauma and you found some comfort in psychotherapy; yet, not found what you are really looking for; such as, a deeper desire to understand, wanting a sense of purpose and fulfillment, then I may be able to help.

Psychotherapy has limitations. It sees man as a biological creature and cannot really see man as subject to Cosmic Laws. Psychotherapy may attempt to repair a man, but goes about it without understanding the essence of human nature.

Within all of us is there is a deep need for certainty, happiness, and fulfillment. Man is born into a hostile environment, and most of us are traumatized by our life experience. We do not get the proper nourishment of love, feelings of safety, care, and guidance toward achieving self-approval through the active clear-thinking mind. Consequently, there is a constant feeling of emptiness and frustration.

Unfortunately, we learn by hearsay and experience how things work and why things are as they are; yet we do not see the truth. We only see the superficial surface of life. We live in our imagination and imagine what we see is true. Not realizing that our vision is limited, we imagine that we and others live by free will and that we freely have the right to choose or not to choose what to do.

The truth is, we all are governed by laws: the law of necessity, the law of self-preservation, the law of inertia, the law of cause and effect, and the law of following the path of least resistance.

Gurdjieff explains that very few people will do the hard work to improve because our nature prevents it. Man wants many things and has many desires, but he will only expend the least amount of effort to get what he imagines will make him happy.

This is learned behavior: we learned from other people that we should be able to get whatever we want while making the least effort. How do we break this cycle of counterproductive attitudes when we are conditioned to be like our parents or emulate their negative behavior?

What can the work of Spinoza and Gurdjieff do to help us? What is there to learn and why will only a few want it?

Spinoza's aim and goal is to arrive at a new awakened and fulfilled character by becoming aware of the union that exists between the mind and the whole of nature. You may not yet see the connection, and my goal is to help you understand.

This task is not to be taken lightly. It is your life, and you should take it seriously as if your whole being depended on it.

This kind of work is for the individual who is dissatisfied and wants something beyond what he has experienced thus far in life. It will fuel the search for something deeper and more meaningful, providing him with a genuine purpose and intuitive knowledge that the path is fulfilling.

Improvement of the Understanding

In the piece "On the Improvement of the Understanding," Spinoza says that there are three levels of human knowledge. The first is hearsay, the second is reason, and the third is intuition.

Most people live at the first, and lowest, level. They only see life through the five senses: sight, sound, taste, touch, and smell. Sight and sound become dominant as our primary source for perceiving images that exist in reality. Consequently, man only gathers a limited range of information in the quest to preserve his existence.

This is the sad state of affairs for most of humanity. There are over seven billion people on this planet and most do not realize that this limited perception of reality causes so much of their pain and suffering. Relying upon the five senses might be enough to preserve one's existence, but never to achieve a life of deep meaning.

Reason is a higher level of perception which helps us clearly see how things are made and connected to one another. It helps us see the causes and effects of things, and then infer an idea from other ideas.

For example, what is the idea, the nature, or essence of a cell phone? It is communication. In ancient times, there were runners who carried messages from one area to another on foot. Some Native American tribes communicated across long distances using smoke signals. The invention of the telegraph in the nineteenth century led to a cascade of developments leading to the modern wireless devices we use today. All of these examples express the idea of the desire to communicate.

Man's intellect keeps asking, "Is there another way, a better method to accomplish the goal?" And yet, even men who rely on reason alone can be guilty of excessive pride in the same way that people on the lowest level remain totally blind.

Yes, the rational men who unlock nature's secrets for practical use imagine that they have free will by expressing their genius in the material realms.

These men remain ignorant of a deeper reality: that God or Nature is the cause of all that exists, whose infinite and eternal attributes are as magnificent as they are profound.

God's Attributes

From His infinite and eternal nature, we humans are part of two of God's infinite and eternal attributes: thought and extension.

"Thought" is the infinite intelligence that expresses infinite understanding.

"Extension" expresses all that exists in the physical universe.

We humans are a mode – a part of these two profound attributes.

A mode is a finite entity that stems from something else. Our mind, when it has a clear thought, expresses the attribute 'Thought' and in turn our physical body expresses the attribute 'Extension.'

The mind and body act as one: the mind is the idea of the body, and the body is the object of the mind.

Our five senses collect information from the outside world. When it is affected positively or negatively by external events, a change occurs. We experience a modification in the state or power of our body, perhaps feeling that we have the power to act, or feeling diminished and unable to perform our intended activity. No matter what the outside stimuli is, whenever we react our power is either increased or decreased, aided or constrained. We do not, cannot remain unaffected.

Even though man has made advances in the physical and material world. Great discoveries in science, medicine, electronics, and mechanics; however, it is evident that man has not made any advances emotionally and psychologically. He is quick to anger, to hate and to kill at the drop of a hat. Road rage, wars, and domestic violence are common; little has changed in man's nature.

If you love science fiction and have watched the *Star Trek* movies and TV series, they endeavor to tell us something about what is possible two hundred years into the future. Despite traveling in a space craft at warp speed in search of intelligent life throughout the galaxy, mankind has not matured emotionally or psychologically.

In the twenty-third century, he is still at the mercy of his emotions and often reacts with instinctive anger and hate as he endeavors to destroy his perceived enemy – whether with sharpened spear or hi-tech laser weapon.

In the infinite and eternal universe, there are no forces of absolute good or evil, right or wrong. There are only the eternal laws of nature that direct and effectively influence all living beings by their immutable attributes and constraints.

The law of self-preservation. The law of necessity. The law of cause and effect. The law of inertia. The law of following the path of least resistance.

We humans cannot escape these laws, just as we cannot escape the flaws in our inherent nature.

The Nature of the Work

The idea of our work group includes the teachings and philosophy of Spinoza and Gurdjieff. Its purpose is to learn how to be open and face our nature without judgments.

This process is about learning how to effectively journal the events that trigger us in order to learn how to identify specific emotions such as desire, pain, hate, anger, envy, hope, and fear.

This journaling process can awaken the more advanced part of our mind – that higher level of intelligence which is a conscious and awakened state of our being which loves to improve its power of understanding.

The method of awakening our intelligence is a deliberate step-by-step process. It will dramatically change the direction of your being and your life from a semi-conscious state to an awakened intelligent state.

This is a true alchemy of change!

Spinoza's Language

It will take time and deliberate effort to understand Spinoza. The meaning of his language, his assertion that everything follows from the laws of nature, and that these laws govern and directly influence us.

The laws: Self-preservation. Necessity. Cause and effect. Inertia. Following the path of least resistance.

These laws explain that we are doing the best with the knowledge that we acquired since infancy, such knowledge programmed and conditioned us to act in a way to help preserve our existence and to survive.

We also learned by hearsay and experience, while still believing that we had free will and free choice. And the whole time, we remained unconscious of the reality that this freedom is an illusion.

Spinoza makes an important distinction when he says that while we are conscious of our desires, we remain unaware of their causes. Therefore we cannot grasp how they determine our existence and our fate. Going further, he says that evil is anything that prevents the mind from understanding.

Spinoza's aim, and the goal of this work, is to help people transcend these limitations to arrive at a new character. How so? By awakening the intelligence, endeavoring to improve understanding, and eventually realizing that we are truly intelligent spiritual beings.

However, in order to achieve this we first must learn how to see our nature objectively – without fear or judgments. We must have the courage to get in touch with our pain, frustrations, anxieties, feelings, and emotions, and then examine how they are triggered by everyday events.

You may be twenty or seventy years old without having ever really looked at yourself objectively. But it's never too late! As Socrates proclaimed, the greatest knowledge possible is to "know thyself."

This is the spirit of our work: to awaken and activate the mind.

Spinoza explains in his *Ethics*, "In certain cases the mind is active, and in certain cases the mind is passive."

The active part is when the mind is thinking clearly. Its effort is to understand – it knows when it has achieved clarity and truth. It grows by examining and reflecting upon the challenges, emotional states, and complications that our ego-personality gets caught up in.

The passive mind is comprised of confused and fragmentary information. Its thoughts and ideas perceive reality partially and inadequately. Interestingly, this facet is also where the personality-ego thrives and becomes the material for conscious spiritual growth.

The ego-intellectual knowledge here is also comprised of fragmentary information – the ideas are confused and inadequate. It believes in free will and free choice. At this level of knowledge, the individual will always feel doubt, uncertainty, and lack a true connection with the self. The ego is a shadow of the true self.

We never learned how to really examine or question our thinking, our beliefs, and our habits. Since infancy we were influenced and programmed by those who raised us – we followed blindly, imitating and emulating their attitudes and behavior. We agreed unconsciously, without questioning or offering any resistance.

This is truly passive thinking, if it can be called thinking at all.

But now…

We may not yet be awake, but we're seeking!

A Poem: "Mysterious Path" by Frederick Kettner

Mysterious is my path: who knows its root and flower?
How little I know even to this hour!
Blessed is the intuitive man,
though clouds mar his sight;
one thing alone he feels
he nears the source of light!
This is the summit of truth,
of all great truths the best;
the ascent to it is steep,
the valley beyond is rest.
Thou canst not find thy goal
in book o' theory;
lo, one day thou shalt find
its wisdom dwells in thee!

My Thoughts

During the 1930s and '40s, Dr. Frederick Kettner wrote philosophical and spiritually oriented articles and poems. His writings were published and shared all over the world. He had hundreds of students, and changed many lives for the better.

My teacher, Mr. Gregory Grover, shared these poems with me and his students, and I found that Kettner's words helped restore a sense of purpose and meaning to my life, especially during times when I felt overwhelmed and lost.

Gregory Grover Teacher

I will forever pay tribute and be grateful to my late teacher, Mr. Grover. He allowed me to participate in his group at the Spinoza and Gurdjieff Center, which was originally formed in West Hollywood, California, and eventually moved across town to Santa Monica.

The first two years we focused on Ouspensky's book about Gurdjieff's work, *In Search of the Miraculous*. During the '60s and '70s Gurdjieff was very popular, and there were many Gurdjieff discussion groups around the Los Angeles area.

Gregory Grover attracted hundreds of individuals, mostly young men and women, who sought something from life other than the normal pursuits. We were in search of something deeper and more spiritually enriching.

Most people are attracted to money, fame, career, relationships, family, and entertainment. These desires and goals become problematic when seeking something different and new, because a person can only have one primary focus at a time.

The imagination is tantalized by exciting material things, wealth, prestige, money, fame, as well as family, tradition, and the pleasures of the senses. When these pursuits are at the center of a person's daily life, then spiritual awakening and growth inevitably must take a back seat.

Attracting New Students

My teacher Gregory Grover found that studying his students' natures provided a treasure trove of spiritually orientated revelations. He began to write and record messages which the public could call in and listen to. These insights over time turned into an impressive body of work.

We loved Mr. Grover's recorded messages, and eventually asked if we could compile them into a book for future study. He agreed, and these recordings were converted to essays and published for private use. Many years later, after Mr. Grover had passed away, I decided to share this work with my students and the public.

The book is called *How to Solve Life's Problems*. To learn more, visit my website WayofSpinoza.com and click the Resources tab. Scroll down to the cover and click the link – it will take you directly to Amazon.com. You may also want to purchase *In Search of the Miraculous* and Spinoza's *Ethics*.

The information contained in these three books lays the foundation for what you will need to follow my lessons. They teach the process of awakening our true intuitive spiritual intelligence.

I find that Gurdjieff is easier to read than Spinoza, and provides a great introduction to the work that I do. His ideas about psychology and human nature are insightful, powerful, and ultimately congruent with Spinoza's ideas.

The following is one of many essays that Gregory Grover wrote, and which I use to help my students begin to grasp the magnificence of Spinoza and Gurdjieff's ideas on human nature.

Essay: "Being a Student"

How do you know things?

A great deal of our knowledge is based on hearsay. Much of what we believe and value comes from our parents' opinions and beliefs.

Are you a student of your own nature?

This is totally different from being a student of things outside yourself. To study math or chemistry is vastly different from studying oneself. Very few people are interested in studying themselves, and therefore very few people grow.

I shall give you an example. Harold required a statement from his father's accountant as a partial requirement for obtaining a contractor's license. He asked the accountant what he would charge to prepare the statement, and the man replied, "Not much."

But to his surprise and anger, Harold later received a bill for $125 despite the document preparation being such a small amount of work.

Harold called his father to complain, and although the older man agreed that the accountant's charge was too high, told his son, "If you have learned a lesson from this, the money will have been well spent."

Harold's father had in fact expressed this sentiment on several previous occasions, but Harold still had not learned anything from these experiences.

I suggested to Harold that he write about what had happened as a way to really study his own nature. Because even though he had already paid $125 for a course in the school of life, if he didn't actually learn anything from it, that money would have been wasted – and in the future, he would have similar experiences over and over.

Harold needed to force his mind to consider new ideas. Memory does not help in these situations, because in this storeroom there are no answers.

There is in all of us, as in Harold, a tremendous amount of mental inertia. To deal with problems concerning our nature, we must overcome far more of this inertia than when thinking about things outside of ourselves and to which we are not emotionally involved.

You have probably heard the saying, "Those who do not learn from history are doomed to repeat it."

I would add that this holds true for personal history as well as world history.

Comments

You may have already intuitively grasped the deeper meaning of what my teacher was expressing here. It is the idea of being a student of your own nature for the purpose of coming to a new character.

What does that character look like?

Experiencing a deeper sense of self. Feeling confident and speaking in a bold new way. Having the courage to express and stand up for your principles.

It is a great feeling to let go of the fear of what other people think about you. Then what will follow is freedom, peace, and happiness.

Carol Case Study

Carol was a student of mine for over four years. She initially contacted me when her son Ted was using heroin – she was in immense pain, suffering shame and embarrassment and feeling like she had failed as a parent. She was at her wit's end.

When Carol came across Spinoza's work, she saw that he was a clear thinker and wondered if she could improve her own thinking in order to positively influence her son. She searched for Spinoza on YouTube and came across my videos, then decided to contact me directly for help.

After hearing Carol's story, I suggested she purchase an excellent book by clinical psychologist Dr. Shefali Tsabary called *The Conscious Parent*. It explores how parents are unaware of their own baggage and blind spots while relating to their children, often blindly leading them to confusion and fear.

I found the case studies in this book important and relatable to help understand how our lives were shaped as children by unconscious parents. Dr. Tsabary's work is compatible with the work that I do.

As we studied *The Conscious Parent* together, Carol began to cry when particularly affected by certain passages. She was drowning in pain, regret, shame, and self-judgment. Judgments prevents us from really seeing, questioning, and examining ourselves.

When I observed that we could not focus properly while she was crying, Carol gathered herself and put forth a new effort into the ideas we were studying.

She discovered that she was dwelling in the past. But we cannot change the past, and I suggested to Carol that she should examine her nature and see what we can do about improving the present.

Carol believed that if her thinking improved she could change her son. I reminded her that my focus was to help her improve her own understanding – how she applied that was up to her own efforts.

Within six months Carol was showing signs of improvement, and several months later her son Ted emailed me and thanked me. He noted positive changes at home, including his parents not arguing and fighting anymore. There was a new lively energy in their home.

Carol was an enthusiastic and dedicated student. We looked at her background, including her relationships with her mother, father, husband, and how she related to her adult children.

Her daughter Sue was always a good girl, did everything to please her mom and dad, got excellent grades, did her homework, and helped with chores. Conversely, Ted was rebellious and began taking drugs as a teenager.

When Sue graduated from high school with high honors, she was featured on the front page of the local paper. As Carol was proudly reading about her daughter's success, a neighbor came to the door very concerned. There was a story on page two about how Ted – including a photograph of him stealing a carton of cigarettes from a local market.

Carol's pride and joy about Sue's achievements were

crushed by being mortified about Ted's criminal behavior. Carol still felt the pain of that day during our time together.

We experience desire every day, and we automatically feel pain when we don't get what we want. This is a basic fact that follows from the law of self-preservation and the law of necessity.

What follows pain is hate and what follows hate is anger. We are all conditioned to believe that hate is bad. Whether through religious teachings or by our parents, we are told that we should not hate anyone. And yet, we still feel hate.

The definition of hate: hate is pain accompanied by the idea that someone else is the cause. We experience pain when we feel rejected, diminished, or restrained, and when our desires are not met or realized. The painful feelings are of powerlessness, helplessness, impotence, and not knowing what to do.

However, writing in your journal activates and awakens the higher part of the mind, our true intelligence. The mind begins to reflect upon itself, its thoughts, and begins to question the ego-state of confusions. It endeavors to examine the emotions, the situations that trigger the ego and its reactions.

Anger is desire to remove our pain, but ultimately, we should also want to understand our pain. When we feel powerless about a situation and do not know what to do, we must surrender to this state and see the value in accepting it. This is supremely difficult, almost impossible to do without guidance.

Eventually, our awakened intelligence can apply the tools of reason and intuition because it loves to improve its understanding by working on problems. It knows that when we put new efforts to any challenge, the mind begins wondering what is possible, what can be done, and begins to address the problem by putting in further effort.

We start simply by trying anything that shows us putting in more effort than before... and then something amazing will happen! Countless new questions and ideas will flow towards us. For now, it doesn't matter what we do with these new feelings and emotions – as long as we acknowledge them, this awakens the mind on its journey toward enlightenment.

But remember, if we ignore this cascade of new concepts and feelings, the passive mind will automatically bury them. When we ignore or buffer this truth, it could lead to depression, anxieties, and physical illnesses. Freedom is achieved by facing our problems and seeking to understand them.

Carol Factualizing

Carol learned the value of factualizing her confusions. She began to recognize her desires, and when these were not met, she would feel pain, then hate, and then anger.

As we have seen, the definition of hate is pain accompanied by the idea of an external cause. Anger is desire whereby through hatred we are induced to remove or destroy the object of our hate. We will do whatever is necessary to eliminate that source of pain from our lives.

It follows the law of necessity that we want to run away from or remove our pain as quickly as possible. We all run from pain and seek pleasure. This is automatic and there is no free will or free choice in the matter. We are under the illusion that we freely makes decisions. In truth, we are only aware of our immediate desires and remain unaware of the underlying causes which determine so many of our actions.

If we cannot face or confront the person we believe is causing our pain, we will automatically run or walk away from them. Consequently, we also instinctively gravitate towards whatever we perceive as pleasurable. But this pleasure will only serve as a temporary fix while seeking to escape our pain.

In journaling, we must acknowledge that we do not have free will in such circumstances. When our mind begins to see and understand this truth, we learn that we are unconsciously following the law of necessity. This is a sleep state or a semi-conscious state of being.

Therefore it is so important to have a teacher and mentor who has been through this process. By yourself, as Gurdjieff would say, it is impossible to wake up. There is no way to test your clarity, or appraise your ideas, and it is too easy to lie to ourselves. When we imagine that we have reached a high level of spiritual consciousness, we experience feelings of euphoria that are as misleading as they are temporary.

I asked Carol to sit with her pain and ask herself, "What is this feeling of pain?"

She wrote down the following:

"I feel pain, I feel powerless, I feel helpless, I feel impotence, I feel worthless, I really do not know what to do."

As you can see, this is exceedingly difficult but extremely important to do. Eventually, as you sit with yourself, surrender to your feelings, not judging, just being... It will awaken the higher mind, your clear intelligence. You will begin to sense a new effort is required and encouraging ideas may suddenly come to you.

"How can I face this challenge? How can I solve this problem?"

There will be good feelings as you put in the effort, with a new sense of 'I' and a higher level of being manifested as you repeat this process over and over.

To help Carol further understand this process, I suggested that she go to my website, WayofSpinoza.com, click the blog tab, then scroll down to the Louis C.K. post titled "On the Meaning of Being Empty." In the five-minute clip, where Louis is interviewed by late-night TV talk show host Conan O'Brien, he relates the importance of facing one's pain and sitting with it.

Allow the pain to settle in, embrace it, try not to run from it. Surrender to the feelings it contains. Then a miracle will happen.

Louis C.K.

Louis C.K. is hilarious in this segment called "Louis C.K. Hates Cell Phones." He's talking about his resentment toward the cell phone because it distracts people from talking to each other. This can be a problem when the cell phone becomes a form of entertainment or constant distraction. It can become an obsession if we spend hours on it each day.

Louis C.K. made an important discovery. He realized that the cell phone is also an escape from our inner pain. We rely on it to avoid our fear of being alone and feelings of emptiness. We constantly need to be busy, with something or someone to occupy our time.

Being alone makes us realize our emptiness and we do not want to go there. We run from this pain of loneliness and seek the cell phone to escape.

Louis C.K.'s anecdote was an excellent example of what I am trying to communicate here about the importance of acknowledging and surrendering to your pain. By wading into this emptiness, then good feelings will come and fill that void.

Louis C.K. is in touch with this good feeling. However, he really does not understand that the good feelings arise when our minds are active, when that desire and effort to understand is awakened. As you feel the joy of understanding, this pleasure is immense, and you want even more of it.

If you do not immediately get that feeling, don't worry, it will come in time and with more effort and experiences. This is a process that must be repeated over and over. First and foremost, you must acknowledge and surrender to your emotional pain.

A good feeling is more than just a momentary sense of well-being. It is part of the process of waking up the mind in its effort to understand. This part of the mind that can be awakened loves to see the truth, because truth brings a feeling of completeness, of wholeness, and feelings of joy in having the courage to face our painful confusions.

The awakened intelligence loves this; it is the true spirit of our mind to understand. After each new positive life experience, we want to repeat this process over and over because it strengthens the mind's understanding.

But remember, understanding is the muscle of the mind. The process of improving understanding requires constant effort and active involvement. In time we learn to trust this process, as our nature develops a whole new sense of self.

We will develop more confidence, have more courage, and begin to sense the true spirit of our nature. Personal power and potential are waiting to be unleashed!

Carol Embracing Spinoza

Carol's increased power of understanding had a positive effect on her son Ted. She recently received a poem from him on her birthday and I asked if she would allow me to share it. I wanted to give other people the opportunity to see how this work has changed Carol's life and how you too can experience dynamic growth in mind and spirit once you embrace the effort.

Ted's Poem to His Mom

My mom is the most important person
Not in the world, or of the world,
but OUTSIDE like a star
You'll always be within me shining in my heart
You do not know how strong you are
You didn't from the start
So many stars up in the sky twinkling in and out
If I could aim to be like one,
It's you without a doubt
You've seen and felt so many wrongs
And your journey has been far
Yet still your kindness shines without
to people in the dark
My favorite conversations and connections
are with you
You have an inner beauty and endless courage
To put up with the fear and hate
that sometimes is inside
I want to give you more respect, Mom!
I love you, keep doing what you do.
Ted

Factualizing and Journaling

The importance of journaling and factualizing is that it facilitates a process of awakening the more advanced part of the mind – our awakened intelligence.

It really is possible to free ourselves from hate, envy, anger, jealousy, and fear. You just need to follow a step-by-step method of going slow and making the effort repeatedly until it feels right. You might be surprised how simple this turns out to be.

First, your intention must be to write about the experiences that trigger your feelings and emotions, such as anxieties, frustrations, anger, resentment, and stress. Begin by writing about the event, situation, or circumstance that caused your negative reaction. Then reflect on what you actually wanted to happen – what were your desires and expectations?

Say you had planned to get together with a friend you hadn't seen for a while and wanted to catch up. You were supposed to meet at a local coffee shop, but you waited for thirty minutes and he or she never showed up. Your desire was not realized, and you felt dismissed or rejected. This would instantly cause you to experience pain, and from pain you will automatically feel hate, and that hate will trigger anger.

I've been told by many of my students that they do not believe they feel hatred, because in our society hate is perceived as worse than being angry. But for now, just trust in this process while we break the event down.

You did not get what you wanted. Your desire was not met. Naturally you were upset. Can you now see that hate is not that big of a deal? It simply means that we feel pain and believe that someone or something has caused it.

Are you beginning to see the cause and effect relationship of how your emotions direct your life? If not, review this over and over, and eventually the active thinking part of your mind will be engaged.

Again, I want to emphasize that there are two parts to the mind: the active thinking part, and the passive part that is confused and relies on memory. Our ego thrives in this passive memory state. It operates through the lens of past experiences. It believes that we have free will and freely choose every decision we make.

The active part of the mind is a dynamic thinking state of being. It lives in the now, in the present moment. It sees the reality of nature. It sees the truth and flows with the laws of nature. It knows that we obey the law of necessity and the law of self-preservation and that free will is an illusion.

This process of awakening the intelligence will take time to understand. Fortunately, the awakened state of being thrives in the process and always desires to improve its understanding.

Definition of Pain

We have said that pain is a decrease of power – it can also be seen as a state of less perfection.

Perfection, according to Spinoza, is synonymous with reality. Consequently, the more reality means the more perfection. As the mind increases its powers through reason, we can act and partake of living and functioning in the present reality. Being truly in the now.

Here's an example. Let's say you're working on a report for your job or for school. Things are going as planned, when suddenly the computer freezes up and shuts down.

You will automatically feel pain and get angry. If you are highly emotional you may even start swearing or break things. If you are highly intellectual, you will feel paralyzed or get depressed. Both reactions tell us that you are no longer participating actively in life. You have no power to act rationally and solve your problem in the moment.

The work that we do is to learn how to face these types of problems as they arise. However, we must learn how to assess our behavior without judgment, which is difficult to do. Begin by freeing yourself and renewing yourself through honest efforts. Write down your feelings of being powerless, feeling impotent, and not knowing what to do.

When you commit to this process, you'll find that it builds mental and emotional strength.

Being in Touch with Our Pain

Pain is associated with feelings of powerlessness, helplessness, emptiness, impotence, and not knowing what to do. If you can stay with your pain, embrace it, surrender to the feeling and be with it throughout your whole being, a miracle will happen. You are now in touch with truth.

Most of the time we run from pain. We want to escape from this feeling, escape to something pleasurable. It can be alcohol, drugs, food, gambling, or pornography. We gravitate towards these pleasurable pursuits to escape from our true feelings. The pleasures we initially seek to buffer our pain may lead us to pleasures that later become excessive. This is how addictive behaviors form.

Again, this is all automatic behavior, there is no free will here or free choice – it is compulsive, repetitive behavior. If we run from our pain like this, we will always remain egoistic and passive, semi-conscious machines. We become the victim of circumstances and harbor the belief that life is suffering.

We even lament that God is not fair and ask how God can allow suffering in the world. Imagining God as an anthropomorphic being, or a personal God, is another illusion rooted in our memories and self-centered thinking.

Problems of Addiction

The retired Hungarian-Canadian physician Dr. Gabor Maté is on a mission to communicate what he has learned from the field of medicine and his own efforts to understand the body-mind connection. He gives lectures and seminars, some of which can be found on YouTube.

During his wide-ranging career, Dr. Maté worked as a pediatrician, GP, and treated patients addicted to heroin. He came to the conclusion that while most drug users have recreational habits, there are certain common personality traits among people with the propensity for addictive behavior.

Dr. Maté's work on the body-mind connection is often rejected or ignored by his peers in the medical profession, such as in the area of family clinical psychology. Fortunately, other fields of the health service industry do embrace his theories.

I think psychiatry and the neurological medical fields would benefit greatly from Dr. Maté's work. But there is a problem in medicine, in science, and in the field of psychiatry: they follow hard rules, accepted protocol paradigms that were established many years ago and are now unquestioned patterns of diagnosis and treatment. Everything is learned by rote, memorized robotically, and without seeking a deeper understanding of the information available to them.

That is why these industries dispense drugs so freely. They can only see man as a biological creature and are unable to understand that he is also a part of cosmic law.

The so-called average doctor does not understand the body-mind connection. Medical students only learn to observe a patient's symptoms, isolate a single condition, and then recommend a specific medication to treat it.

But medication oftentimes has side effects. Even when a patient voices concerns, the doctor replies by asking what is worse, the painful condition that you are experiencing or possible the side effects?

This mechanical thinking about the human body is what doctors learned during their education. Unfortunately, the emotional and psychological aspects of human nature are ignored. Despite the medical student's many years of training, his bedside manner still leaves much to be desired.

The pharmaceutical industry also has a tremendous influence on how medicine is practiced in this country. Doctors are tempted with incentives for prescribing new products, hospitals receive donations, free samples are offered, on and on. It's common sense to see that this presents a major conflict of interest.

God forbid if people were actually healthy in their daily lives and didn't need to see a doctor or go to the hospital.

Perfection and Reality

Spinoza explains that pain is less perfection itself, where perfection is synonymous with reality. Therefore, if being in a state of pain detaches us from reality, then our power is decreased while trying to handle the problems before us.

The sequence then follows a predictable pattern: When we are overwhelmed, the situation is beyond our capacity to deal with. Consequently, our inability to take action is evident.

Now you are starting to recognize the pattern: Our desires are not met. Pain follows automatically. The law of necessity and the law of self-preservation dictate our behavior.

If we use this example of a friend who did not show up for a meeting, we go through the emotions of pain, hate, and anger. No one chooses this type of reaction, and it is repeated over and over when our desires are not realized or met. We have no choice. We are a victim of circumstances.

The force of nature expresses itself. It does not choose, but bestows its laws upon all living things. There is no good or bad in nature – it just is.

Fortune or failure falls upon every level of human nature. Nature does not discriminate between the good and the bad. Man is blind to the realities of nature, and he is only aware of his desires and needs. Man does not have free will or free choice – he only imagines that he does.

Belief in free will is a major cause of why our emotions are triggered by everyday life events. We are aware of what we want, and yet oblivious to what causes our desires and how they determine our existence.

There are many things that trigger us and cause emotional pain. These painful feelings are trying to communicate to us that we lack the power to face the situation or problem before us. When we feel powerless to do anything about it, then we feel like a failure, experiencing shame and embarrassment.

Pain is really saying to us that life is challenging us to put in more effort to get the things we want. Life is a school: the school of hard knocks. We must go beyond our normal level of effort to meet these challenges. We can learn a great deal by doing what is required.

We resist because man lives in an imaginary world of "should" and "should not." He expresses stubbornness, buffers, and procrastination. These are necessary behaviors because they follow beliefs, habits, and attitudes.

As children we learned by example to give the minimum effort to get things done. If we cannot solve a problem, we give up easily. Here the laws of inertia and of following the path of least resistance manifest, and we remain in a painful, suffering state.

We learn how to operate in the world by example. If our environment was passive – meaning that our parents were inefficient, unfocused, absentminded, and put in the least amount of effort to get whatever they wanted done – then we will do likewise.

I have a close friend named Gloria. She's an amazing woman who grew up in a family that demonstrated love, caring, discipline, and taught her the importance of applying herself to everything she did.

Gloria went to college to study business, then earned her master's degree in education. She worked in the wine and spirits industry, and being the only female salesperson when she started out several decades ago, she became extraordinarily successful.

However, her story is extremely rare. For most of us, our parents were neglectful, fearful, unloving, demanding, and judgmental. This kind of environment weakens the spirit of the child whereby the parent is not able to share love, give intelligent guidance, or nourish us. We end up with feelings of emptiness and loneliness, living our lives in a desperate state of neediness.

Importance of a Teacher

When I joined the Spinoza and Gurdjieff study group, my teacher encouraged me to go beyond the present level of my efforts. Whenever I had a feeling or a partial idea prompted by one of his questions, he suggested that I apply my mind and elevate the feelings to a clear idea so that he and others could understand what I was endeavoring to communicate.

The idea of applying mental effort while facing the daily challenges I was confronted with has radically changed my life and increased my ability to think rationally. As I continue to review and reflect upon the concepts explored in Spinoza's *Ethics*, the power of my understanding has dramatically improved through the use of both reason and intuition.

Consequently, the idea of myself has changed greatly, powerfully, and spiritually.

Resistance to Change

One major roadblock to understanding is that we are not aware of how we assimilate new knowledge. It is so easy to imagine that we instantly grasp a new idea and say, "Oh yes, I get it."

We do not realize that we don't actually study very deeply, but instead skim over books ever so lightly. This is superficial because we are in a hurry to get the information.

Envy, ambition, and competition are motivating factors that drive us. We have an immense amount of information already stored in our memory from collected experiences, thoughts, images, beliefs, attitudes, habits, and premises. We do not really examine any of this and have vague feelings about the material and books we read.

Consequently, we tend to automatically assimilate any new material into our worldview without trying to understand that new knowledge. We are stuck in a rut with all the old stuff crammed into our memory banks. It is impossible to grasp new information if our identities are so beholden to the old.

We do not know the difference between thinking and memorizing. It is so easy to imagine that we understand a new idea. Unfortunately, mostly we just gather information and connect it with other things we're familiar with. We are similar to a dictionary in that we have a lot of ready information at our disposal, but don't realize that it is just data without context or application.

The Process of Transformation

To increase the power of understanding we must learn how to observe our nature without judgments. Therefore, in creating a new reality, you must learn the value of factualizing. So slow down, take out your journal, and write down your feelings and emotions.

We are easily triggered by events and circumstances that do not go our way or when our desires are not met. Learning to get in touch with our feelings and emotions and writing them down in a journal will begin stimulating and awakening our intelligence.

The active awakened mind is our true intelligence. As you journal magic will happen. You will begin to feel lighter and freer. By focusing on your frustrated mental state – that is, your pain, hate, and anger – and journal about the situation that triggered you, you will begin to find clarity and turn your thoughts away from what you perceived as the cause of your pain.

Remember, when our desires are not met, we feel pain automatically. We focus on what we perceive as the cause, blaming the person or thing that prevented us from getting what we wanted. The process of factualizing begins by learning how to write, to journal about the event that caused our pain, and specifically examine what it was that we wanted, what it was we desired.

Try not to judge yourself while writing down your feelings. Journaling helps to separate our emotions from what we perceive as the cause of our pain and instead focus on new and deeper thoughts. Writing stimulates the higher levels of the mind, our intelligence which wants to understand.

Also, write down that we do not have free will (even if you do not yet believe it), and that the other person who harmed you also does not have free will. Why? Because everyone acts from the laws of necessity and self-preservation.

In time you will begin to see and understand that they are not really the cause of your pain and discomfort. When the intelligence is awake, we learn by reflecting upon our thoughts. Then we actually see how things really are.

This is reality: we see what we are doing and being.

"I am confused. I am being hateful. I am angry."

To get in touch with your being is the beginning of how to change and improve your character. This is a slow and deliberate process of becoming a master of your emotions and a master of oneself.

As you better understand the definitions and the meaning of your emotions, of how they play out and are expressed, then you will begin to taste freedom. The more you understand, the more your mind is strengthened, and the more freedom you experience.

Those who are highly intellectual may find it exceedingly difficult to embrace or even acknowledge that they have emotions. Most intellectuals avoid their emotions because emotions make them feel uneasy and a lack of control.

This can be troubling as they are especially fearful of confrontation, because of the unknown emotional possibilities and fear of powerlessness. Normally, intellectual types feel superior to those who act more emotionally. Most attorneys, doctors, scientists, engineers, software programmers, and coders live within their intellectual center. They tend to fear social gatherings and are unable to emotionally connect with people.

Unfortunately, they may also feel alone and isolated. They retreat into what they do best, immersing themselves further within their professions and fields of expertise. Some become workaholics in order to avoid emotional pressures at home.

Gurdjieff talks about three centers that express man's being. First is the intellectual center. Second is the emotional center, and third is the physical center. Everyone has all three, yet one is dominant in each of us.

When I first met my teacher at the age of thirty, my emotional center was dominant while my intellectual center was very weak. Even though I was a successful hair stylist and salon owner, I felt inferior intellectually. Eventually, while working with my teacher, I began to see my true nature and grasp Gurdjieff's ideas about these different centers within man.

I accepted that my emotional center was the dominant force in my being and my intellectual center was weak. It was apparent to me while trying to follow a set of instructions to assemble something that it would trigger my frustration, pain, and anger.

The new awareness of this reality then helped me control my emotions when faced with intellectual challenges.

Emailing with David

The following is a conversation I had with a man named David over the course of several emails:

Dear Lewis,

I have been going through Spinoza's *Ethics* recently, and I came across a proposition in Book II, about how God or Nature is a thinking thing, or in other words, thought is an attribute of God's Nature. What do you think Spinoza meant by this? That Nature thinks in the way humans think? That Nature has some form of consciousness? What did he mean by thought? Could he have simply meant patterns and laws? If so, why did he use the word thought? I appreciate your response.

-David

Dear David,

Good questions. In Spinoza's language, Nature or God consists of infinite attributes. We are a part of two, an infinite and eternal attribute of "Thought and Extension." The attribute "Thought" expresses the infinite understanding and intelligence. When the mind of man is in touch with his active clear-thinking mind, this is an awakened state of being. This can only come about because we are a mode of this thing's nature, his attribute "Thought."

The spirit of man is his mind. In proposition 1 in part 3 of the *Ethics*, in the proof, Spinoza explains that God constitutes the essence of our mind. Meaning we are thinking with the mind of God and are clear and have an adequate idea. To understand this, you must awaken your mind, your essential intelligence.

   -Lewis

Dear Lewis,

Thank you very much for your response. But I am unable to see how understanding and intelligence in any way exists without the specific structure of the brain. After all, Nature does not possess any structure of a brain such that humans do, and events in Nature simply unfold according to the laws of physics without any understanding or intelligence being involved.

How could understanding or intelligence be associated with the Earth's gravitational attraction to the Sun? Isn't it simply governing laws which dictate this interaction? Perhaps I am missing something, I just don't rationally see how consciousness can be an "infinite and eternal" attribute of Nature.

   -David

Dear David,

May I ask, how did you become interested in Spinoza? How did you find me? What are you looking for? Do you work in any of the fields of science? I know what your difficulty is. To answer your question, I need a little info from you. Is that okay with you?

   -Lewis

Dear Lewis,

I became interested in Spinoza's *Ethics* through the writings and quotes of Einstein, who was deeply influenced by the 17th century thinker. When I picked up the *Ethics* and tried to read through it, I was taken aback at Spinoza's assigning thought or intelligence to everything in the universe, which to someone like me who was educated in the sciences, I find distasteful. So, I thought I'd read more interpretations about Spinozism, and came across your site. Yes, I am a biomedical engineer.

-David

Dear David,

You being a biomedical engineer tells me that you are highly intellectual. Your intellect favors reason, facts, figures, and scientific proofs. It is interesting that one of the most respected and acclaimed theoretical physicists was Albert Einstein. He is quoted as having said, "My God is the God of Spinoza."

What did he understand and mean? Then another question might arise, "What is God?" Einstein understood and agreed with Spinoza that in nature, cause and effect is apparent. Yet, in quantum physics cause and effect is dismissed.

Primary elements such as protons or electrons do not follow cause and effect. They occupy one space and then another at random. As you can see, I have an extremely limited understanding of science. Many years ago, I purchased a book called *Understanding Physics* by Isaac Asimov. On the first page he said that we must forget and dismiss intuition because intuition is not a science.

Spinoza was called a heretic and an atheist. His books were banned during his lifetime due to the fact that he dared to spread his idea that the Bible is not the work of God, but of men. He said that the Bible is a way to curb man's appetite for excessive behavior. A book of morality only.

Spinoza's philosophy includes science, medicine, and mathematics. The *Ethics* was written in geometric form to prove his ideas and explain them in a way that would help the reader understand.

However, you can see how difficult it is to follow and comprehend. I have a limited formal education, yet I understand much of Spinoza. Prior to the five parts of the *Ethics*, Spinoza includes an essay called "On the Improvement of the Understanding."

In this part, Spinoza explains his method how to improve our understanding. You might say, "Well, I have a good mind and I can see through reason how things are put together. Yes, I have a scientific mind. Therefore, I need proof!"

Spinoza brings out a very important reality that the scientific community overlooks and dismisses. The significance of intuition. Spinoza's intuition is not just a deep feeling, it is a knowing, a deep recognition of truth. Spinoza explains that when we know we have a clear idea, we know it. There is an affirmation of a clear concept that the mind knows. It does not require proofs!

Why are you having such a difficulty? You must acknowledge that you do not understand and that you want to understand. You may already have determined what God is, if you were influenced by a religious upbringing. If you embrace science, because science embraces reason that measures and compares things, you conclude that there is no God because God cannot been seen or measured.

Einstein is a good example. He bypassed the accepted rules and paradigms within the science community during his time. He found that his mind was far above conventionality. It has taken over a hundred years to prove Einstein's idea of gravitational waves. He saw it yet did not actually prove it. So how could he see it, was this intuition?

Science wants to prove things, to verify. Yes, this seems reasonable, yet it is limited. To see what Einstein saw and what Spinoza understood, you need intuition, which according to Spinoza is the highest level of knowledge.

The first level of knowledge is made up of hearsay and experience. The second level is reason. The third and highest is intuition. Intuition sees clearly, directly, and knows with certainty the truth. When the mind is clear it knows the difference between itself, the imagination, falsity, and fictitious ideas.

I might be able to help you, that is, if you are open to it?

-Lewis

Dear Lewis,

Thank you very much for your reply. I appreciate deeply that you took the time to respond to my concerns. Currently, though, I'm simply not open to any sort of teaching, but thank you. I wish you all the best.

-David

Overview of David's Interest

As you can see, David is highly intellectual. Individuals who are intellectual can become a surgeon, attorney, biochemical engineer, astronaut, businessperson, etc. Yet this knowledge does not change his nature or his being.

As Gurdjieff explains on page 65 of the book *In Search of the Miraculous*, an individual may have great knowledge, but that knowledge cannot change his being.

Then what is being? Being expresses the character of the individual. Everything in him. His likes, dislikes, expressing love and hate, how he can be charming and deceitful, expressing mindfulness and narcissism, being caring or resentful. All this expresses the being of the individual.

Intellectual knowledge which is directed towards educational achievements has to do with a career, profession, title, position, etc. However, it has no power to change one's inner character, that is, his emotional and psychological nature.

The highly intellectual person believes that he has a great mind and feels superior towards the less fortunate.

Yet he feels inept in other areas of his nature, such as an inability to feel his emotions – if he ever does, he quickly suppresses them and is afraid of them.

He may feel inhibited and fearful of social gatherings. Scientists, engineers, and other intellectual types do not do well with small talk, so-called meaningless talk. They fear intimacy, closeness, and touching.

An intellectual interested in studying Spinoza has an inferiority or superiority complex and desires to prove Spinoza wrong. If he cannot grasp Spinoza's ideas, he quickly dismisses him.

The intellectual is prideful and has exaggerated beliefs concerning his mental powers and abilities. He is unconscious or semi-conscious about the fact that he lives and operates by the law of necessity; meaning, that he follows what he understands and is directed by the desires that were programmed and is now stored memory.

He has no free will or free choice.

Gurdjieff "Personality and Essence"

On page 161 of the book *In Search of the Miraculous*, Gurdjieff explains:

"It must be understood that man consists of two parts, 'Essence and Personality.' Essence is in man is what is his own. Personality in man is what is 'not his own.' Not his own, what has come from outside, what he has learned."

The personality expresses the ego state – it is a false sense of self. However, we need our ego because it is necessary and an important part of our lives to survive and exist. Our ego is formed by the environment we grew up in, where we were exposed to so much information about how to live, exist, and function in society.

The ego believes that it has free will and free choice; however, this is an illusion. The ego uses the body's five senses: touch, sight, taste, smell, and hearing. The body gathers information from its senses. The mind is aware of the body's affects by the images it perceives.

I want to add that the mind is the idea of the body; consequently, whatsoever occurs in the body, or when the body is modified or affected, the mind has an idea of such affects.

The mind and body work as one, yet they are modes of two distinct attributes: the attribute of thought and the attribute of extension, expressing the infinite Being's nature or God.

The body and mind's perceptions of reality are limited. We do not really see clearly. It is as if we are looking through dusty, chipped, broken lenses. We develop false premises, then come to beliefs without clarity and judge automatically.

For example, consider when we see someone from a different culture, different skin color, and who speaks a different language. We may judge that person as evil just by association or hearsay. Perhaps an authority figure, someone you highly admire and respect, says that a certain class of people is evil. You will automatically agree and begin to judge those other people and fear them.

The ego lives on the surface of life, its nature is superficial without real substance. It lives in the imaginative world of competition and comparison. Consequently, all negative emotions manifest when we are in our ego state. It expresses in polarities of inferiority and superiority. On the other hand, our essence, meaning our essential intelligence, is an awakened state of being.

You will learn on page 84 of my teacher's book *How to Solve Life's Problems* that it is deeply insightful, both psychologically and spiritually, and can become a gateway to activate your intelligence, your true essential nature. This is an awakened state of being. We begin to learn to understand; in this process of awakening, everything we learn from this state of being is our own. This cannot be taken from us.

As Gurdjieff explains on page 163 of *In Search of the Miraculous*, "Our personality and all its confusions are the material for our essential nature to grow."

Belief in Free Will

There are over seven billion people on this planet, and everyone believes that they have free will and free choice.

Spinoza explains that we are conscious and aware of our desires, but unconscious of the causes of our desires and how they determine our lives.

May I ask you, if you have free will, why can't you change your depression or sadness to being happy? Can you free yourself and change addictive behavior willfully? Or free yourself from excessive use of drugs, pornography, or food just by your will to do so? Can we willfully be happy all the time? Can we be confident just by willing ourselves to be so?

Spinoza explains that true freedom is understanding how our nature works and to understand the laws of nature that influence us. What are the laws of nature? The basic laws that affect human nature are the law of necessity, the law of self-preservation, the law of inertia, the law of cause and effect, and the law of following the path of least resistance.

The law of necessity tells us that of everything which exists in nature, both animal and human nature will do whatever it can to exist, persist, and preserve one's being with the knowledge they have. This comes from the lowest level of knowledge, called hearsay and experience.

Since infancy, we are influenced by our parents, guardians, religions, the news, books, and schools on how we are supposed to be. From all these sources we learn what is right and what is wrong, good and bad, how to speak, and what to believe in. We are like sponges, and then we copy, emulate, and imitate those around us. We follow their beliefs, attitudes, habits, negative patterns of thinking, and prejudices.

This is all necessary to help us learn to exist and preserve our existence. As a child we need nurturing, love, shelter, security, and food. We are totally dependent emotionally and psychologically. As we get older, we all want to belong, have friends, and be popular; we do not want to be lonely.

The belief in free will is deeply rooted in our psyche and includes the belief that happiness is something that comes to us from outside. It can be material things, such as money, fame, and the pleasures of life. This is the basic cause of our misery. We have no idea how to nourish our inner being, our essential nature.

Gurdjieff "Magnetic Center"

I first heard of people having a magnetic center from Mr. Gregory Grover as he explained Gurdjieff's teachings. Grover, who was my teacher for over twenty years, explained that within man there are great possibilities of becoming a master of oneself and his emotions. This idea attracted me deeply.

Throughout the years I observed that many students who were exposed to my teacher's wisdom came and went. Both women and men, they sometimes stayed for months or years before eventually leaving. It puzzled me why anyone would walk away from this truth that my teacher was communicating. Only many years later did it finally dawn on me why people leave work of such a miraculous nature.

Gurdjieff talks about a magnetic center that is within us. Some have it more than others. Some do not have it at all. This magnetic center is our intuitive nature. It knows the truth when exposed to it.

I applied myself for years trying to understand Spinoza. It is a very difficult process. In spite of my resistance, I found that I needed to apply more and more effort to comprehend these most difficult ideas as communicated by my teacher.

Ouspensky's book *In Search of the Miraculous* is based on Gurdjieff's ideas, and at first was difficult to comprehend. Spinoza's *Ethics* meanwhile was impossible! But over time, as my level of effort increased, the desire to understand my nature in relationship to Gurdjieff and Spinoza's teaching increased.

There is a force in me, a strong desire to grasp what Spinoza was communicating in his *Ethics*. As my understanding increased, I realized why people give up the work and leave the group.

It is because most do not have an intuition that is strong enough to understand Spinoza's *Ethics* and its significance. They are not dissatisfied enough, and they are overwhelmed by life's distractions. Their desires are stimulated and lured away by the forces of nature.

Again, I repeat, we are governed by the forces of nature, and we do not have free will. Most individuals will not take the time or apply the great effort required to do the work.

Gurdjieff explains that to awaken from a deep sleep much is required from us. Unfortunately, most people feel they know what will make them happy, such as a relationship, sex, sensual pleasures, fame, wealth, a career, etc.

Before someone can awaken, they must first be extremely dissatisfied with where they are and not find anything in life that brings true happiness and fulfillment. They must want more, believe that something is missing, or feel empty. They may sense that clarity and truth are possible and want that something which can enrich their inner being and essential nature.

I think most of my peers were not really dissatisfied enough, and they got tired of all the time and effort that this work requires. They were satisfied with superficial things that gave them some basic sense of happiness, even if it is only temporary.

This work helps us to differentiate between our ego-intellectual nature, which is in a semi-conscious state of being, and which relies on memory while believing that it has free will and is the cause of its desires and actions.

The awakened intelligence is our true essential nature. Unfortunately, most students quit the work too soon, and never get in touch with their true intelligence, that awakened state of being.

We must intuit that it exists, and we must want it desperately.

The Mind

Spinoza explains that the mind is a thinking thing, it is intangible and not a physical entity. The brain is not the mind, it is the storehouse of information for our memory. Everything that we do, have done, heard, believed in, imagined, and experienced is stored in our brain. The brain plus the spinal cord and the gut regulate all systems of the body. These include the immune system, lymphatic system, circulatory system, electrical system, skeletal system, etc.

Spinoza, in part three of the *Ethics*, explains in proposition 1 that "our mind is in certain cases active, and in certain cases passive. Insofar as it has adequate ideas it is necessarily active, and insofar as it has inadequate ideas, it is necessarily passive. Proof: In every human mind there are some adequate ideas, and some ideas that are fragmentary and confused. Those ideas that are adequate in our mind are also adequate in God, insofar as he constitutes the essence of our mind."

Spinoza explains that at times our mind is clear, and we understand. At other times, we are really confused and do not know or understand. The awakened state is an active part of the mind and the sleep or semi-conscious state is the passive part. The active part wants to understand. It is the intelligent thinking part of the mind, and it lives by reason and intuition.

The passive part of the mind is comprised of confused ideas. It is our ego state and depends on memory and it believes in free will and free choice. Mankind suffers and lives in pain because he does not know the reality, the causes and the effects, and the nature of things.

For example, we are aware of our desires but unconscious of how those desires influence and determine our action. Our desires are easily stimulated, so that we might suddenly find ourselves doing something we regret, such as overeating, gambling, drinking to excess, etc. Our desire can lead us to addictive tendencies.

As Children

Let us consider the environment we grew up in. As children, we are programmed to be competitive and are always comparing ourselves with others. We live by our emotions, such as hope, fear, envy, pain, hate, anger, and more. Our emotions tell a story of how we are affected by what we are seeing. How are we relating to and handling the challenges that life throws at us?

We are easily stimulated when our desires are triggered by the forces of nature, and when our desires and expectations are not met, we will automatically feel pain.

Again, may I remind you, Spinoza indicates that human nature follows from the laws of necessity and self-preservation. The ego-self cannot see or understand this truth, because it has a false sense of self. It is only a shadow of who we can potentially become. However, our ego is necessary in that it exists. It is a part of self-preservation, and it expresses all of our desires and emotions.

As a young man, Spinoza saw and wanted all the things that were supposed to bring him happiness, such as riches, fame, and the pleasures of the senses. He began to see that those things did not help him attain lasting happiness.

Do you remember the pleasurable experience of buying a new car? It had that fresh new smell, and was just so beautiful! Eventually, as time passed we lost the feeling we had when it was still new.

Yes, these things that seem wonderful at the time, but happy feelings do not last. This is what I found to be true: that my true fulfillment and salvation was not found in the things that I normally desired. Anything of real substance can only be understood intuitively and with a high level of reason.

Peace, happiness, and fulfillment are possible for all of us. Therefore, I continue working to improve my understanding and be intuitively connected with the source.

Free Will

There are over seven billion people on this planet and most believe in free will. I am sure you do, too. I did, we all do. It is universally accepted. We are born into this belief and that is what it is, belief!

For example, Bob has a friend named John. John borrowed $30 from him two weeks ago and has promised to pay him back by Friday, but is now avoiding Bob. Bob needs this money so he texts daily, but John doesn't respond.

John has a pattern of borrowing money from friends and not paying his debts. Even though he has a job, he spends everything he makes and literally cannot hold onto money. The idea of budgeting is not in John's vocabulary. He does not know what budgeting really means.

Bob believes that John purposely and freely chooses not to pay back the $30. Bob believes that John should behave differently from what he is, and expects to be paid back. Bob is now angry, feeling pain and hate.

This example explains how we do not see clearly: we only see the surface of life. Believing in free will, we are not able to see the cause and effect of things.

What is taking place is that nature follows from these laws:

1. The law of necessity

2. The law of self-preservation

3. The law of cause and effect

4. The law of inertia

5. The law of following the path of least resistance

These laws are an expression and a manifestation of Nature, that is, the Infinite power of Nature or God.

As you can see, you may have a reaction. You may think, "Of course I believe in free will, everyone does," and you are right. You may also think that you have a choice and have the free will to be an atheist who does not believe in God. Notice how you resist new information that is so contrary to your belief system. It is impossible to embrace new ideas when we our mind is full of preconceived notions. You never questioned what you were told, heard, or experienced. You absorbed and accepted information without question, this is passive knowledge.

Spinoza has a method in his *Ethics* that explains how to differentiate between clarity and confusion. There are two parts to the mind, an active thinking part and a passive confused part. As Gurdjieff would say, the passive mental state is the sleep or a semi-conscious state that expresses our nature. The awakened thinking mind is the active part, and it is our true intelligence.

Comprehending this is a process that takes time, patience, and effort. The results are amazing.

Case Study: Laura Next Door

There are things that affect us which trigger our emotions when our desires are not met, when we feel restrained, and when we feel rejected.

An emotion is an idea in the mind that we are aware of our body being affected or modified When we see or hear something that makes us feel pleasure or pain, an idea forms inside the mind which expresses how our body has been affected. If we feel pleasure we feel an increase of power; if we feel pain there is a decrease of power.

Case study: Laura lives in the apartment next to me. She has a mild case of dementia and sometimes doesn't know who I am, even though we dated several years ago.

Problem: Laura knocks on my door several times a day. She may ask for help finding her keys or want me to help operate the TV controller.

This is what works in me:

- I feel pain
- I feel hate
- I am angry

I believe Laura has free will, and I believe I have free will.

I called the building manager and he told me that management cannot do anything. He advised me to call the police.

I called the police, and they came and talked to Laura. She told them that she doesn't remember knocking on my door. The police said that the situation is management's problem, so they cannot do anything.

Again, this is what is operating in me:

- I feel pain
- I feel hate
- I am angry

I believe Laura has free will, and I believe I have free will.

We want to understand the nature of our emotions:

Pain: is less perfection, feeling powerless, helplessness, and not knowing what to do. However, we skip this reality and go directly to hate.

Hate: is pain accompanied, connected, and associated with the idea of an external cause. Our focus is on the thing that triggers our emotions. We also believe that Laura has free will and free choices. We take her actions personally.

Anger: is desire whereby through hatred we are induced to destroy the object of our hate. In other words, we want to remove what we perceive as the cause of our pain.

As you begin to examine and look at each emotion and learn the definitions and their meaning, it will stimulate your mind to think. This is a process of awakening the advanced part of the mind, our true intelligence that is directly connected with reason and intuition.

As you continue the factualizing process this will develop in you a new sense of self, and you will begin to embrace your understanding. The force and power of the understanding is to improve and strengthen itself and come to clarity. This will bring you self-approval, self-love, and a path towards happiness.

We must get back to our initial response when your desires are not met or realized. Pain is a feeling of powerlessness, helplessness, and not knowing what to do. You want to embrace these emotions and feelings, surrender to them. Just like Louis C.K. embraced and surrendered to his feelings of loneliness. He cried like a baby, then good feelings followed because he was true to himself.

Chapter 42, "Objective Self-Observation," on page 84 of my teacher's book *How to Solve Life's Problems* will help. Also, for more clarity, go to page 248 in the *Ethics* and reflect upon propositions 2, 3, and 4.

In our anger, we want to get in touch with our fantasy and imagination of what we would like to do to the person who we imagine caused us pain. "I want to throw

Laura off the third floor balcony. I want to destroy her. I want her to disappear." The more you are in touch with your pain, hate, and anger, the more freedom will be possible.

I want to emphasize this is a long-term process to free ourselves from being a victim of our emotions. The more you experience situations that trigger you when your desires are not met, you will automatically express the same emotions over and over.

But power lies in our understanding. Growth is possible when we understand.

Love and self-approval follow.

Pain is a decrease of power, or less perfection. Perfection according to Spinoza is synonymous with reality, meaning that we able to face the problem in the moment, we are facing reality. Consequently, the more reality the more perfection.

As the mind increases its powers through reason, we are able to act and partake in living and functioning in the present reality, the now.

For example, you are working on a report for your job or at school. Things are going as planned until suddenly the computer freezes and shuts down.

You will automatically feel pain and get angry. If you are highly emotional you may break things, start swearing, etc. If you are highly intellectual, your mind will freeze or get depressed. Both reactions tell us that you are no longer actively participating in life. You have no power to act rationally and solve your problem.

The work that we do is to learn how to face such problems. In doing so, we must also learn how to look at our behavior without judgment, which is difficult to do. Begin to free yourself and renew yourself with new efforts. Write down your feelings of being powerless, impotent, and not knowing what to do. Doing this will help you learn to face the problem with renewed effort. This process builds mental strength.

Being in touch with our pain is a feeling of powerlessness, helplessness, emptiness, impotence, and not knowing what to do. If you can stay with your pain, embrace it, surrender to the feeling and be with it with your whole being. Then a miracle will happen: you are now in touch with truth.

Most of the time we run from pain. We want to escape from this feeling, escape to something pleasurable. It can be alcohol, drugs, food, gambling, or pornography. We gravitate towards these pleasurable things to escape from our true feelings, such as not knowing what to do, feelings of helplessness and powerlessness.

The pleasures we seek buffer our pain and may lead us to habits that become excessive. This is where addictive behavior is automatically formed. Again, this is all automatic behavior, there is no free will here or free choice, it is repetitive compulsive behavior.

If we run from our pain, we necessarily remain in our imagination as egoistic, passive, semi-conscious machines. We become the victim of circumstances and harbor the belief that life is suffering, and that God is not fair and how can God allow suffering? Unfortunately, we falsely imagine God as an anthropomorphic being, a personal God.

Mind and Body Connection

One of my students suggested I look at Dr. Gabor Maté, a retired MD who has also written several books and now lectures. He was once featured on a TED Talk and you can also see him on YouTube.

I think his studies and ideas complement what I do, so I have incorporated Dr. Maté into my studies of human nature and how man can learn to free himself from his past and improve by awakening his intelligence, the active thinking part of our mind.

The following is taken from page 59 of Dr. Maté's book *When the Body Says No*:

> For seven years, Michelle had a lump in her breast. Periodically, it grew or shrank, but it never caused her or her physicians any concern.
>
> "Then all of a sudden it got really hard, got hot and started to grow almost overnight," the thirty-nine-year-old Vancouverite says.
>
> A biopsy revealed that the tumor was malignant, and Michelle believes she knows why: stress.
>
> "It wasn't until I shocked the hell out of my life that it changed," she says. "I quit my job, without any income to go to. ... My emotional state was horrible at the time. A lot of things hit me all at once, not only financial."
>
> Michelle had a lumpectomy and was relieved to learn that her lymph glands were free of cancer. The surgery was followed by chemotherapy and

radiation, but no physician ever asked her about what psychic stresses she might have suffered before the onset of her malignancy or what unresolved issues she had in her life.

When the Body Says No

Here is another case study taken from page 22 of Dr. Maté's book *When the Body Says No*:

> The gifted British cellist Jacqueline du Pré died in 1987, at the age of forty-two, from complications of multiple sclerosis. When her sister, Hilary, wondered later whether stress might have brought on Jackie's illness, the neurologists firmly assured her that stress was not implicated.
>
> Orthodox medical opinion has shifted extraordinarily little since then. "Stress does not cause multiple sclerosis," a pamphlet recently issued by the University of Toronto's MS clinic advised patients, "although people with MS are well advised to avoid stress."
>
> The statement is misleading. Of course stress does not *cause* multiple sclerosis—no single factor does. The emergence of MS no doubt depends on several interacting influences.
>
> But is it true to say that stress does not make a major contribution to the onset of the disease? Research studies and the lives of the persons we have looked at strongly suggest that it does.

Such also is the evidence of the life of Jacqueline du Pré, whose illness and death are a virtual textbook illustration of the devastating effects of the stress brought on by emotional repression.

My Comments on the Book

The book is fascinating, and I highly recommend it. What I see in these examples is the reality of how human nature is shaped by the environments we grow up in.

In Jacqueline Du Pré's case, she was forced by her mother to forgo childhood to be a friend and caregiver to her mother. Jackie was groomed to please and suppress her own feelings of pain, hate, and anger.

For individuals who repress their feelings, the negative effects may manifest in different ways. When we are triggered and are unable to express our anger or hate, there is a buffering mechanism that is built into our psyches that stops us from experiencing our feelings.

Is it from our free will and freedom to choose? Are some children brought up to be perfect little machines without feelings and emotions? Should we not express hate because hate and anger are bad?

In these case studies, Dr. Maté explores human nature, its totality in mind and body. Unfortunately, modern medicine does not see the mind-body connection. This disconnection gives us an overview of the weakness of so-called modern medicine. Assuming that there is no real cure for cancer, heart disease, and diabetes, then treatment becomes a one-size-fits-all way to deal with the problem.

I want to add that what Dr. Maté is missing is the reality that all living creatures live by the laws of nature, and particularly the laws of necessity and self-preservation. Man does not have free will or free choice.

Did Jackie du Pré willfully want to suppress her feelings? Why couldn't she express them? It was necessary that she do so, and she did her best with the knowledge she had. Her knowledge of her own nature was confused and lacked understanding of how she was being; that is, the emotional and psychological aspects of herself.

She never questioned her thoughts, her beliefs, and patterns of behavior. She was basically like a robot, a semi-conscious human being acting mechanically, and doing whatever she was told.

The environment she grew up in was indeed stifling and weakened her mind and spirit. However, due to her musical talent, she did become a world-famous cellist. It is evident that her suppressed feelings and emotions were openly expressed with full passion when she played. Her performances had an immensely powerful effect when audiences listened to her play.

Medical Field Lacks Understanding

On page 59, Dr. Maté says:

> Breast cancer patients often report that their doctors do not express an active interest in them as individuals or in the social and emotional context in which they live. The assumption is

that these factors have no significant role in either the origins or the treatment of disease. That attitude is reinforced by narrowly conceived psychological research.

Emotional Disconnection Causes Cancer

On pages 59-62, Dr. Maté continues:

> An article in the *British Medical Journal* reported on a five-year study of more than two hundred women with breast cancer that aimed to determine whether a recurrence of cancer can be triggered by severe life events, such as a divorce or the death of someone close. The authors concluded that "women with breast cancer need not fear that stressful experiences will precipitate a return of their disease." Dr. Donna Stewart, a professor at the University of Toronto and chairwoman of women's issues for the University Health Network, commented that the study's results "made sense."
>
> Yet Michelle and the many other women who suspect a strong relationship between stress and their breast cancer have science and clinical insight on their side.
>
> Research has suggested for decades that women are more prone to develop breast cancer if their childhoods were characterized by emotional disconnection from their parents or other disturbances in their upbringing; if they tend to repress emotions, particularly anger; if

they lack nurturing social relationships in adulthood; and if they are the altruistic, compulsively caregiving types. In one study, psychologists interviewed patients admitted to hospital for breast biopsy, without knowing the pathology results. Researchers were able to predict the presence of cancer in up to 94 percent of cases judging by such familiar psychological factors alone.

This is an example of Dr. Maté expressing intuitively how the nature of the mind and body work together and how one affects the other. There is an inner knowing of the nature and causes of things.

In Spinoza's philosophy, it is so important to include the emotions in studying his most deep and difficult concepts, and why intellectualizing alone cannot grasp the wholeness of human nature.

Evidently, we must include the desire to understand and love of our efforts to understand.

The Unconscious Parent

I have also included Dr. Shefali Tsabary in my studies as she complements the idea that man and woman as parents are asleep and unconscious as they endeavor to parent their children.

The following case study is a prime example of a parent wanting perfection from their child. It appears on page 44 in a chapter called "The Ego of Perfection" from her book *The Conscious Parent*.

Most of us harbor fantasies of perfection, but it's our attachment to such fantasies that keeps us from flowing with how our life really is.

For instance, when a mother planned her son's bar mitzvah, she spent over $30,000 on the arrangements, perfecting each detail. Despite the fact she had fussed for months, she was nevertheless extremely anxious when the day arrived.

As it turned out, the occasion was punctuated by what this mother saw as disaster after disaster. ... [She] noticed that her son had become somewhat tipsy and was being rowdy in front of her relatives and high society friends.

We all identify with what we have, what we do, how we look, our status, and our level of education. We are so concerned with trying to impress others, to appear perfect in their eyes.

Everyone desperately needs external approval, but why? Because we lack it! However, there is an innate need, an inner requirement for approval that must be satisfied.

Spinoza explains that self-approval through reason is the highest level of being one can hope for. Through the effort we make to improve our understanding, and the process of learning about our nature, self-approval is earned.

We feed our being through the effort of improving our understanding. Throughout this book, as you research and reflect, you'll discover Spinoza's method of awakening your true intelligence through reason and intuition. It is possible to improve our understanding and it is through our understanding that we gain a true sense of self, which is totally different from the ego-intellect that relies on memory.

Our understanding is an active thinking state of being that lives in the reality of the now, the present. Our ego state relies on memory and is past-minded. It lives in comparison and competition, seeing what is not rather than what is.

The active mind lives in the reality of the present, in the now, and loves to apply itself. It learns to exert effort in solving problems and gains strength through these endeavors.

The ego avoids problems and puts in the least amount of effort. It expects that things should come our way easily with minimal effort. There is deep inertia in the human mind resistant to change and improving its thinking. It relies on hope that things will turn out the way we want and fears that they will not.

Spinoza's Ethics

If you're interested in reading Spinoza's *Ethics*, I recommend the Elwes translation released by Dover Publications. There's a direct link to this product on the Resources page of my website, WayofSpinoza.com. Used books are cheap and in good shape.

In the *Ethics*, you will discover how the mind works, what God is, and learn all about the emotions, of human bondage, and the idea of coming to freedom. Also included is a most important introductory essay called "On the Improvement of the Understanding."

Spinoza has given us a method of strengthening our mind by improving its understanding through the use of reason and intuition.

Spinoza's God

Spinoza was called an atheist, yet everything about his *Ethics* expresses God's nature. So much so that some people perceived him as a God-intoxicated man.

What is God? Most religious groups believe that God is an anthropomorphic being, a personal God sitting on a throne like a king while dispensing punishment and favors to people.

Spinoza published the *Theological-Political Treatise* in 1670 and caused an uproar. Why? Spinoza had studied the Bible for several years trying to see if it contained anything that would explain God's nature and His wisdom. But he found nothing and came to the conclusion that the Bible was the work of men and not the work of God – a text of morality, but not absolute truth.

Consequently, Spinoza was looked upon by the clergy as a heretic and ostracized by the Jewish community. He had dared to say that it was no longer necessary for Jews to claim that they were God's chosen people, and that God's nature was to be embraced by all people equally. No religion had any special covenant with God nor the authority to rule over any other religious faiths.

The belief that one religion is superior to others and

favored by God is one of the main reasons that man destroys man. Competition and comparison, the desire to be superior, is probably the main cause of war between different groups of people.

Mankind lives by his senses and emotions. When his desires are not met, pain is the result. Pain is a feeling of impotence and powerlessness. What follows pain is hate and what follows hate is anger. This is all automatic, a robotic semi-conscious state of being.

While we are aware of our desires, we remain unconscious of their causes and how they determine our existence. Mankind lives at the lowest level of knowledge, which is informed by hearsay and experience. There is no rational or intelligent reasoning. To understand God's nature we must apply the higher levels of knowledge through reason and intuition.

It may be possible through determined and intense efforts to learn Spinoza's method in improving our understanding and come to a whole new character. Then we will experience what it means to be truly born again. This new character clearly knows itself and its emotions. Consequently, we become consciously aware how we are part of Him, that is, Spinoza's God.

Spinoza explains that God is a being that expresses infinite and eternal attributes. We are a part of two, the attribute "Thought" and the attribute "Extension." We are a mode, that is, a modification of these two attributes. This is very difficult to understand and it took me several years to grasp. Fortunately, I have devised a method so that it will take you only a fraction of the time. My desire is continuing my own personal growth while sharing with you all the promise Spinoza suggests in his *Ethics*.

Knowledge and Being

Gurdjieff's core ideas were chronicled by his student P.D. Ouspensky in a book called *In Search of the Miraculous*. While I do not resonate with everything that's in this book, I do focus on the parts that involve human nature while avoiding the material about octaves, planets, and body movements. His insights into human nature truly are profound and complement Spinoza.

Spinoza understood that human nature follows from cosmic laws and that free will is an illusion. However, if you read pages 65-67 of Ouspensky, you will also sense the significance of Gurdjieff's insights about human nature.

He says, "People understand what knowledge means, and they understand the possibility of different levels of knowledge. They understand that knowledge may be lesser or greater of one quality or of another quality. But they do not understand this in relation to being."

What is the being of man?

My Comments on Gurdjieff and Being

You can see how difficult it is to comprehend a new language. Gurdjieff explains that general knowledge does not change the being of the individual. By general knowledge we mean that you may have the professional knowledge of a neurosurgeon, a lawyer, a nurse, or businessperson. But none of this career information can change your being. You may ask, then what is being?

As Gurdjieff explains on page 66, being is his character, everything in the individual, his whole character. He expresses love, hate, courage and fear, clarity, confusion, compassion, contempt, love, hate, strength, and weakness. All this makes up the being or character of man.

Therefore the goal and aim would be to seek how to change our being. Spinoza explains in "On the Improvement of the Understanding" that he wanted to come to a whole new character. What does that character demonstrate? "It is the knowledge of the union existing between the mind and the whole of nature."

Spinoza is talking about a new character that is achieved by deeply knowing oneself, by examining our emotions and putting forth the effort to understand.

For example, what causes pain and how do we free ourselves from emotional and confused states? By increasing the power of our understanding, the intelligence is truly awakened. In this awakened state we understand intuitively that we are a part of His Divinity and there is a union that necessarily exists between our mind and His eternal and infinite intelligence.

This is where I want to introduce the poems of my teacher's teacher, the late Dr. Frederick Kettner. His collected works, *Back to the Nameless One*, express a potential of living from our intelligence, which in turn expresses the spirit of man as connected with the infinite understanding.

Poem: "Wait with Rejoicing"

Why is it that men quarrel and hate each other that confusion is theirs?

What kind of world is this? They come together without understanding or

knowledge of bliss. Freedom men crave, but slaves they become.

Who arranges this? Ask thou mayest always, wait, wait for the answer,

till thy soul is awakened. But wait for it! Wait! Within is the answer.

From thy soul it will come, today or tomorrow, unaware as an angel.

With rejoicing await it. That answer will come! Oh, wait with rejoicing.

My Comments on the Poem

While a student of Gregory Grover, I read this book of poems often and took time to reflect. They offered me solitude from the chaos and challenges of working as a hair stylist and salon owner.

Intuition is Necessary

Spinoza and Gurdjieff communicate a different language of clarity and truth. Gurdjieff says that man is asleep, and while it is possible that he can awaken, only a few will make the effort to improve their being.

"Man is asleep and only a few will want to do this work, because their being prevents it."

Why is this so?

I think people are too busy pursuing what they think is important, such as riches, fame, success, career, material wealth, and satisfying their various pleasures.

While Gurdjieff does not go much deeper in explaining how to awaken the mind, his general premise offers amazingly insightful ideas about human nature. I know from my own experience, having done this work for many years with an increased power of understanding, that what Gurdjieff communicates is true.

However, to understand these concepts, intuition is necessary. Logic and reason alone are not enough. Spinoza's *Ethics* also offers a method of awakening the mind that will help us come to wisdom and understanding. Unfortunately, most people miss this reality. Those who study Spinoza want to read the *Ethics* like a mass-produced novel, and only after applying minimal effort do they realize how frustrating that can be.

You cannot understand Spinoza from a strictly intellectual standpoint. There must be an emotion of desire and love in your effort to understand. When you give all of yourself, your whole being will be profoundly affected as you begin to grasp, assimilate, and live by Spinoza's ideas.

Gurdjieff explains that true spiritual growth is a higher conscious state of mind. You cannot expect to willfully change just by reading, attending a seminar, or just listening. You cannot do this by yourself because it is too easy to lie to ourselves. We imagine growth, not realizing we are fooling ourselves. We are too subjective, too attached to our beliefs, habits, patterns of being, and ways of thinking.

There is a parable spoken by Jesus that says, "You cannot put new wine in old bottles." What did he mean? That you cannot put new ideas into a mind that is full of confused thinking and beliefs.

Gurdjieff expresses the idea that we need a teacher, or someone who has gone through the process of awakening. Someone who is interested in our growth, that can help us, see the truth. Someone who understands where are we emotionally, psychologically, and how we think.

Most people find it difficult to open up to others. We are secretive, judgmental, and feel ashamed. We struggle to admit our failings and weaknesses. We suffer and don't understand what causes our pain.

Spinoza on the Bible

Spinoza studied the Bible intensely for over five years before writing his *Theological-Political Treatise*. He wanted the average person to use reason to free themselves from irrational dogmatism, the church's wrath, and political fears whipped up by the monarchy.

During Spinoza's time, there was constant war and governmental oppression. People lived in ignorance and extreme poverty. He hoped that his ideas would help people use reason to lead more courageous and happy lives.

Unfortunately, Spinoza's books were banned and he was branded a heathen because he dared to say that God is not a personal God and that the Bible is the work of men, not of God. He had concluded that there is nothing in the Bible that explains the nature of God or how to understand the nature of man. But it is a book of morality, a guide on how to live without being a danger to our fellow man.

Despite the scorn he endured throughout his lifetime, Spinoza and his philosophy were rediscovered a hundred and fifty years later by Goethe and other 19th century philosophers. Spinoza's work influenced democratic forms of government and his insights into the Bible opened the door for other thinkers to question its authority. And today, Spinoza is viewed as the father of modern psychology.

Spinoza on Jesus and Moses

Spinoza understood intuitively that while Jesus spoke directly to God mind to mind, Moses spoke to God face to face. What is the difference and meaning?

Jesus understood the nature of God and was able to make a direct connection with the infinite and eternal source while in a highly conscious state. The attribute "Thought" expresses the eternal and infinite understanding and that we are a mode, a part of this attribute.

Spinoza wrote in the proof in proposition 1, part 3 of the *Ethics*, that God constitutes the essence of our mind only insofar as our ideas are clear and distinct. We too, if understood through clarity of thought and adequate ideas, express a communion directly with the being of Nature or God.

Moses saw God face to face. This means he saw an image and heard a loud voice, rather than communicated with God in his mind. Through their interaction the Ten Commandments were born. This code explicitly teaches people how to survive and live morally.

Jesus expressed His philosophical lessons through more subtle parables which require us to find the truth through intuition and reason. These parables speak with great depth to those who can understand.

Spinoza: A New Character

Most readers of Spinoza's *Ethics* find the book difficult or impossible to read, much less understand. Many of my students have had Spinoza on their bookshelf for years. My purpose as a teacher, mentor, and a coach is to help you learn how to grasp Spinoza's most difficult concepts. It takes time, desire, and effort.

Why did Spinoza write the *Ethics*? What was his aim and his purpose?

We will go over the following topics:

1. Pursuit of a lasting and permanent happiness.

2. Spinoza's idea of a new "character."

3. Why man's ordinary pursuits bring about fear, sadness, and despair.

4. The four levels of perception and choosing the best.

5. Learning how the mind works and how to improve its powers of understanding.

6. Knowing truth through reason and intuition.

7. Becoming in union with this infinite being, Nature or God, which Spinoza calls Nature or God.

Next I will take you to the third part of the *Ethics*, "On the Origin and Nature of the Emotions." Why is it so important to know our emotions? In time you will understand that our emotions are the gateway towards clarity and truth.

Over two thousand years ago Socrates expressed that the highest and greatest knowledge is to know oneself. What is there to know? Is it possible to follow reason and control our emotions? Why does man suffer?

Buddha's followers sought a way to rise above suffering, but in my opinion Buddhism only touches the surface. Inhibiting, ignoring, or suppressing our desires by way of meditation in order to arrive to a blissful state is an illusion and can only take us so far.

As Spinoza says, man lives by his desires and desire is the essence of man. Everything manifested and expressed by your being is desire. The need to eat, sleep, have sex, drink, be entertained, feel power, and be approved expresses desire. Desires are the things we gravitate towards, they are what we believe and are conditioned to follow. They also preserve our existence.

What you desire is dependent on your programming. We were all conditioned since childhood to follow our authority figures. We desperately needed to be cared for by others. Consequently, we took on all their habits, patterns of behavior, their beliefs and attitudes. We became just like them with only slight variation.

We come to know our emotions more clearly through a process of factualizing in a journal about the situations that triggered us. We can then acknowledge the specific emotions we felt, such as anger, hatred, fear, pain, envy, jealousy, and pride.

While journaling is not new, I have taken the process to a level that really allows us to get in touch with the deeper aspects of our nature. This process when done correctly will stimulate and awaken your true intelligence and the desire to understand. In time, this effort will lead you to freedom from the bondage of your emotions. As you taste the fruits of your efforts to understand, you will also experience feelings of joy and fulfillment.

This will always be in proportion to your efforts. The more you seek to understand through journaling, the more power and clarity arises, and the more feelings of joy.

Spinoza explains that the more you know your emotions, the more you will know God. Eventually your mind will possess a deeper connection with the whole of Nature, because your mind, through reason and intuition, will become strong enough to see and understand the reality of how we all are a part of the whole of Nature, and of God.

Improvement of Our Understanding

The "Improvement" treatise appears prior to the five parts of the *Ethics*. It is extremely important, and without which it would be impossible to understand the *Ethics*.

This philosophical work lays out the parameters of Spinoza's quest for truth and permanent happiness. He gives us insights into his search, what he wanted, and describes the obstacles he faced. He goes on to explain his method of how to improve our mind's ability to think, and in so doing we are literally improving our understanding. Only then we can comprehend his most difficult ideas as expressed in the *Ethics*.

This is a higher level of effort and consciousness. At this level of understanding we digest and incorporate Spinoza's ideas into our nature. To understand what emotions you are experiencing you must see it in yourself, such as desire, pleasure, pain, hate, anger, envy, jealousy, hope, and fear. Then Spinoza's *Ethics* will come alive in us as we grow intelligently, spiritually, and psychologically.

I must make something very clear: you cannot do this by yourself alone. Many of my past students had Spinoza's books on their shelf for years, but were unable to penetrate or understand his difficult concepts.

But as Gurdjieff explains, it is so easy to lie to ourselves and pretend that we do know and are growing to a higher level of consciousness, when in reality we are only fooling ourselves.

Regarding Gurdjieff

Gurdjieff talks about how knowledge itself cannot change our nature or being. The knowledge must include our emotions and the whole of our nature.

For example, intellectuals who are prideful of their knowledge perceive others as inferior and express contempt towards them. They do not realize that their own knowledge is limited, and therefore their intellectual powers are also limited.

They live in the world of comparison and competition. They may be a successful engineer, attorney, medical doctor, or computer programmer, but still they are unaware and unconscious of their nature. They are blind to the causes of their desires and how those desires determine their existence.

Gurdjieff would say they are asleep. No matter how successful they might be in their careers, they feel isolated, fearful at social gatherings, fear rejection, and desperately want approval and love. They may be cruel and resentful and disconnected toward their children.

Are you beginning to see how accumulating stores of knowledge and information cannot change one's being or nature? At best, you will become a walking encyclopedia reciting factoids like a machine.

On Reason

This is a good place to introduce Spinoza's idea of "Reason."

Reason is beyond logic. When applied, it helps us to follow what is truly best for us and our nature. In part 4 of the *Ethics* on page 201, Spinoza explains: "As reason makes no demands contrary to our nature, it demands that everyone should love himself, should see that which is useful to him; I mean, that which is really useful to him, should desire everything which really brings man to a greater perfection, and should, each for himself, endeavor as far as he can to preserve his own being.

"Again, as virtue (power) is nothing else but action in accordance with the laws of one's own nature, and no one endeavors to preserve his own being, except in accordance with the laws of his own nature, it follows, first, that the foundation of virtue (power) is the endeavor to preserve one's own being, and that happiness consists in man's power of preserving his own being."

My Comments on Reason and Desire

It takes time for the student to be able to clearly see and comprehend Spinoza's concepts. Therefore, in the beginning of our studies, I help walk the student step by step to learn how to see their nature without judgments. To begin to see how we are being. Every day we are confronted with situations and circumstances that affect us unfavorably.

Here's an example of how desires affect our lives.

You're twenty-four years old. A friend recommends you for a job opportunity at their workplace. You are excited about the potential, feeling pleasure while imagining yourself succeeding at the new job and making enough money to move out of your parents' house.

The job interview does not go well. You leave the office with feelings of rejection. Rejection is pain and a feeling that your power is checked, and this painful feeling arises when our desires are not met. What follows pain is hate and what follows hatred is anger.

We all want to feel good about ourselves. We constantly seek approval to affirm whom we are, what we have, and what we do. Everyone seeks pleasure and tries to avoid painful experiences. However, when we are in a painful situation, what do we do? We can suppress our pain, try to escape from it by taking drugs, or find something pleasurable to eat. Unfortunately, we are not really facing our problems.

The process of factualizing involves writing in our journal about the situation that disturbed us and identifying the emotions that were triggered. These are important steps towards freedom.

The goal is to stay with the pain and factualize the circumstances that created the painful state in the first place. Acknowledge and feel the pain, stay with it, surrender and allow the painful feelings to settle within you. This process stimulates and awakens your mind, the intelligent part that wants to understand. Therefore, pain is accompanied with feelings of powerlessness, emptiness, helplessness, and not knowing what to do. A key component is that you must surrender to the pain, feel it, accept it, be with it.

When we understand we apply reason, which helps us to see and enjoy the effort that is required. With intuition, our deeper intelligence is activated. We are now experiencing a new reality: an awakened mind. The awakened mind loves the problems that feed its understanding.

Just like body loves physical exercises which increase its muscle mass, the mind likewise uses life's problems and challenges as exercise equipment to strengthen and improve its understanding.

Our normal ego state complains, procrastinates, and ignores problems. It lives in the past and imagines it has free will and free choices. It applies minimal effort to what it perceives and desires and lives in the world of imagination, competition, and comparison.

All negative emotions express the ego. Ego is a sleep state, or semi-conscious state of being. Its intellect is comprised of confused and inadequate ideas that are derived from hearsay and experiences. This is the lowest and the first level of knowledge.

Gurdjieff explains this very well on page 66 of Ouspensky's book *In Search of the Miraculous*. He says, "A modern man lives in sleep, in sleep he is born and in sleep he dies." Gurdjieff makes it very clear: how can an asleep mental state acquire new knowledge?

I call this a semi-conscious state, where we are aware of our desires but unconscious of the causes of our desires and how they determine and direct our lives. Both Gurdjieff and Spinoza concur that when man's mind is passive he lives as a machine.

Fortunately, the awakened mind is an active intelligence, living in the present and it wants to understand with reason and intuition. It knows a better path and reason is the effort that helps us get there.

Man's Inhumanity

Religion has brought confusion, fear, dissension, and division among people through the world of promoting fantastic beliefs and images that trigger man's imagination, the extraordinary belief that God is an anthropomorphic being, a personal God that governs like a king. It is believed that man is the image of God, and that Jesus, a man, expresses God's consciousness, and is called the Son of God.

Man, believing in free will, judges himself and others, expects others to do what they believe is right, and lives in the world of should and should not. His being is contemptuous, criticizes, complains, and judges what is right and wrong in man. He believes and lives in the world of dogma, prejudice, and competition.

Man unconsciously follows the rules expressed in the Ten Commandments as presented by Moses. Man wants and expects favors and imagines he has a special covenant with God. This behavior is similar to when children fight for attention from a parent.

The history of man's destruction stemming from religious disparities is horrific. Take for example the Holocaust, the Inquisition, and the Christian Crusades. People will continue killing each other due to confused religious beliefs.

Even today in the twenty-first century, we still have ISIS wreaking havoc in the Middle East, forcing communities to follow their ways of worshiping the Koran. Then there are the Western governments which insist that other countries follow democracy and Christianity. They also supply military aid to perpetuate everlasting war, causing great destruction, famine, and death. Millions of people have been displaced and seek safety in other countries.

Human nature does not understand that they do not have free will or free choice. People follow the laws of necessity and self-preservation. Necessity, meaning that man will do whatsoever that is necessary to sustain his existence no matter the cost. Self-preservation is the need and desire to do whatsoever to sustain one's existence with the knowledge they have.

If their knowledge is confused, they will behave confusedly. Again, man's greatest confusion is the belief that he has free will, and that he freely chooses. Spinoza clearly explains the laws that follow Nature's order. We are aware of our desires but unconscious of the causes of our desire and how they influence and determine our existence.

We are unaware, unconscious of how we were programmed through childhood experiences and influenced by the environment that educated us. As children, we learn through imitation and are constantly seeking approval.

The Conscious Parent

Dr. Shefali explains in her book *The Conscious Parent* that parents are unconscious of how they are parenting. They do not see or listen to their children. They see their children as an extension of themselves. They cannot see that the child has the potential of being an individual with their own identity.

Therefore, if we are raised by unconscious and confused parents, we likewise will follow and imitate their behavior. If the environment we grew up in was hostile and traumatic, where anger and violence were expressed openly, we will have the same tendencies.

Another student named Allen thanked me recently. He said that he is no longer an ogre like the angry violent person he once was. Allen grew up surrounded by violence. His father almost killed him when was five years old. He lived in anger and hate. He was thankful to have learned another way to be. He is more patient, experiences flashes of love, and has more understanding through the work of Spinoza.

Being a Teacher

As a student of Spinoza for these past fifty-plus years, I am forever grateful for my own teacher, the late Gregory Grover. He first introduced me to Gurdjieff and eventually Spinoza, and emphasized how their ideas would forever challenge me to keep increasing my understanding.

I still constantly ask myself, how much do I really know and understand Spinoza's ideas and philosophy? "We must be tested in the marketplace," as Mr. Grover would say. We must reflect each day on how clearly we are thinking and feeling.

If one of my students does not understand, I must apply more effort and find a way to reach their mind. If they find it too difficult, I must wait until they become mentally stronger and better acquainted with the methods of improving their understanding.

The new student may learn, if they are open to it, that there are two parts to our mind. Spinoza says on page 130 in his *Ethics*, that in certain cases the mind is active and in certain cases the mind is passive. In time the student's mind is awakened, and in time they begin to comprehend and taste the difference between the ego-intellect (passive mind) that depends on memories, and the active mind that lives in the now, the present reality. The active mind loves working on problems. Studying a problem is food for the mind and strengthens it, just as exercise equipment strengthens the body.

I constantly ask myself, how well am I communicating? Do I see where the student is, rather than see where they should be? That is my challenge. My hope and desire is basic, to find the individual who desires to become a student, who really wants to know themselves, who intuits that a higher character of being is possible for themselves, and sees the importance and significance of awakening the mind.

Once exposed to Spinoza's *Ethics*, in time it is possible to know the truth, and that freedom and clarity are possible. And ultimately, coming to a higher intuitive intelligence and beginning to see one's relationship with the Infinite Being.

As they progress in this magnificent work, they may want to communicate Spinoza's clarity and truth to others, because they know that true happiness is available to all and all can partake in Her Divinity, so that they are fulfilled, experiencing love, peace, and freedom.

Teacher's Essay: "Solving Life's Problems"

The following comes from two books written by my late teacher, Mr. Gregory Grover, called *How to Solve Life's Problems* and *The Delight in Solving Problems*:

The mind has many levels, ranging from very superficial to very deep. When our mind operates at a superficial level, the quality of our life is superficial: we live mainly through our senses and instincts. Our contact with others is also very superficial, and we are guided almost entirely by our emotions. We are insensitive to the deeper hunger for being and are inwardly unfulfilled. We buffer our feelings of not being internally fulfilled. We fill our time with superficial activities, and we see life in terms of symbols and symptoms. Our desires are symbols of what we need inwardly, and we deal with the symptoms of our problems. Our minds are flabby because they are not exercised. Our motivation is to avoid pain and our pleasures are merely offsets to our pain.

To gain truer fulfillment, we must exercise our intelligence (our mind). The disappointments, the problems, and challenges in life are the exercise equipment that offers us the opportunity to deepen our thinking. The nature of problems and challenges we struggle with will determine the quality of our growth. Dealing with physical problems such as a flat tire or being late to work provides useful exercise.

But problems within ourselves and with others (our thinking, our emotions, our values, our motives) are more difficult problems and compel us to open up deeper aspects of our minds. Both levels of problems are necessary for full development of our mind's requirements.

Our motives in dealing with problems, challenges, and disappointments are most important. Are we pain-motivated? If so, do we consider our problems solved when the pain ceases? Are we pleasure-motivated? Then we may be interested merely in offsetting our pain with pleasure, or living only from senses and instincts.

But if we are joy-motivated, desiring to find deeper and deeper fulfillment, we approach our problems with intensity, creativity, and zeal. There is an inner delight in working on, delving into, and solving problems.

Then we understand that the real solution to problems is not in external results, but in the clarification of our thinking.

My Comments on the Essay

You may wonder about the idea that the mind has many levels. It's true, however. This must be understood intuitively as we learn the process of awakening our mind. That is, our true intelligence, its thinking, and its purpose is to understand.

The mind has the potential to increase its powers of understanding. This is the work, to learn how to understand our nature to come to more clarity. Each effort is the effort to strengthen itself. There are unlimited levels of understanding, depending on our mental efforts.

A Lazy Mind

You may see that some of your friends or family members can only think about gaining material things and projecting a certain image of themselves. Most are concerned with where they live, their financial investments, education, social status, what they own, and do for a living.

They have no interest in deeper things that relate to improving your character, about improving your understanding, examining how you are being, regarding your emotions, feelings, and your ideas. This is a higher level of consciousness, a higher level of being that they cannot relate to.

Consequently, you are dismissed, and it is impossible for them to hear you. They quickly change the subject because in reality they are living on the surface of life, a superficial life.

A flabby mind is a lazy mind. When our mind is soft, we do not examine or question anything. We expend the least amount of effort. We are stingy when applying ourselves, and are too lazy to extend ourselves to problems. We procrastinate and avoid facing our problems.

As you see, the above essay talks about working on and solving problems. Unfortunately, we were brought up to believe that we should avoid problems and apply the least amount of effort in whatever we do.

Who wants problems? "I sure don't," we say. Therefore, to gain a true sense of self, our mind must awaken, and once it has awakened it begins to learn the value of working on and solving problems by learning how to increase our efforts. This effort is to understand, and in putting forth this effort, we gain a powerful sense of self and learn to feel fulfilled through this effort. This effort creates self-approval and self-love.

Understanding the Ethics

A few years ago, several of my students complained that Spinoza's *Ethics* is too difficult to understand, and asked if there was a way that I could make it easier for them to grasp.

What is required from us to understand Spinoza's ideas? Why are his concepts so difficult to comprehend?

The problem is not that obvious because we do not realize the level of our own inertia, our resistance to apply our mind. We do not realize that we are automatic robotic machines, that we follow the law of necessity and that we have no free will. This is exceedingly difficult to understand.

You may even ask, "What do you mean I have no free will? That is ridiculous!"

I understand. Just be patient and you will begin to see what is really happening.

We learned very early in our development as children how much effort we would apply to any mental or physical problem that challenges us. Our level of effort emulates and copies our parents and the environment we grew up in. If our parents' level of effort was low, that will be the standard we follow and there is a natural tendency to resist going beyond it.

We are not used to thinking at the level that is required to comprehend Spinoza's *Ethics*. I will go over this again and again. Since childhood we were programmed how to walk, talk, what to believe, our religion was chosen for us, many of our habits and patterns of being emulate our parents, etc.

From infancy to the age of twelve we were obedient children, and then something happened. Natural teenage hormones began to be expressed. We had no choice in controlling our body's biological necessity. You suddenly are interested in sex. You cannot stop your physical growth. You cannot stop your pain and fears just by willing yourself to do so. You cannot force yourself to be happy when you are depressed. You cannot mentally force your mind to will itself to be free from your addictions.

For Spinoza, it was natural to apply great effort in whatever he did. He had learned to put forth this level of effort when he began his studies as a young boy. He was exposed to science, mathematics, philosophy, and Hebrew history.

Studying the Torah required great mental effort. He was being groomed to become a rabbi in the Jewish community of Amsterdam. Great promise and expectations were bestowed upon him.

However, as Spinoza matured he also studied Latin and encountered the great thinkers and philosophers from other societies. He began to question the validity of the orthodox practices, traditions, and habits he had been raised to believe.

Spinoza found the rabbis' interpretations of the Torah to be dogmatic. He thought they really did not understand and stubbornly held onto old beliefs such as Jews being God's chosen people, and that God is a personal God.

He could no longer go along with the traditional identity of what it meant to be Jewish, and instead sought a new quest to satisfy his longing to understand the true nature of God and the achievement of unending happiness.

Understanding Spinoza

There are many books on Spinoza, but in order to follow and understand the work that I do, you must have the *Ethics*. I strongly recommend the Elwes translation.

How did I come to understand Spinoza? I was a member of the Spinoza and Gurdjieff Center, which Gregory Grover created in 1969 in West Hollywood, California. I studied with this group for over twenty years learning and applying the ideas of these philosophers.

In time I began to see and understand why and how these revolutionary concepts changed and improved my life. It took me another twenty years to continue learning how to incorporate Spinoza's and Gurdjieff's philosophy into my life, so I could understand and live by these most provocative, dynamic ideas and teachings.

I wanted to communicate these difficult concepts in such a way that in time you, as a student, will not take as long to understand as I did. I am no scholar, I have no university degree. However, all my learning and understanding comes from my private teacher, by participating in his group, working with fellow students, and using my nature and life experiences.

The wonderful thing is that I still don't understand all of Spinoza. In fact, I'm still learning! This is my life's work, which is to increase and improve my love of understanding Spinoza's philosophy. I'm currently working with several students and the common refrain I hear is, "Why is Spinoza so difficult and why is his material so dense?"

I tell them that we must go slow, going over the material again and again to really learn the language. With my guidance, you will eventually grasp it. But you've got to want it in order to intuit the significance. As your teacher, I have learned how to communicate and explain what Spinoza is telling us.

You must reflect upon the ideas and learn the process of factualizing and identify the intelligent mental state that is so necessary to understand. We must realize there are two parts to the mind, an active and a passive part of our intelligence. Normally, we live by the passive part where the ego-self lives. It depends on memory; it believes in free will and has only a fragmented, superficial idea of reality. All of our suffering and pain is expressed from this ego state.

We must learn how to awaken the mind. First, we must look at and examine our emotions through the process of factualizing the events that trigger our emotions. By looking at and studying our emotions, our mind begins to awaken its active thinking part. We are learning how to see the truth of our nature. Seeing without judgment how we are affected and seeing specific emotions, such as desire, pain, hate, anger, hope, and fear.

Spinoza's philosophical treatise "On the Improvement of the Understanding" is extremely important in helping you to understand this. The "Improvement" is almost like a biography of Spinoza.

On page 3, he begins, "After experience had taught me that all the usual surroundings of social life are vain and futile; seeing that none of the objects of my fears contained in themselves anything either good or bad, except in so far as the mind is affected by them."

You can see by his own experiences what man normally strives for: fame, riches, and the pleasures of the senses. He realizes that those things do not really give us the happiness that is promised. He goes on to explain that he is interested in something that is not transient and perishable, instead wanting something permanent and lasting. Next he asked if there was something outside the normal pursuits that would result in true and lasting happiness.

On page 4, he explains the problems of sensual pleasures, fame, and riches. In fame we see the highest good and the highest desire to reach for, as well as riches. One cannot get enough of both. However, the problem arises when we are in constant fear of losing our level of fame, or so worried about losing our wealth. We become so consumed with these pursuits that we have little room or time for anything else.

On page 5, Spinoza explains, "All the objects pursued by the multitude not only bring no remedy that tends to preserve our being, but even act as hindrances, causing the death not seldom of those who possess them, and always of those who are possessed by them. There are many examples of men who have suffered persecution, even death for the sake of their riches, and of men who in pursuit of wealth have exposed themselves to so many dangers, that they have paid away their life as a penalty for their folly.

"Examples are no less numerous of men, who have endured the utmost wretchedness for the sake for gaining or preserving their reputation. Lastly, there are innumerable cases of men, who have hastened their death through overindulgence in sensual pleasure. All these evils seem to have arisen from the fact, that happiness or unhappiness is made wholly to depend on the quality of the object which we love. When a thing is not loved, no quarrels will arise concerning it, no sadness will be felt if it perishes, no envy if it is possessed by another, no fear, no hatred, in short no disturbances of the mind.

"All these arise from the love of what is perishable, such as the objects already mentioned. But love towards a thing eternal and infinite feeds the mind wholly with joy and is itself unmingled with any sadness wherefore it is greatly to be desired and sought for with all our strength."

I want to emphasize here that you should not to be too concerned with what you do not understand and instead focus on what you do understand.

As you can see and it is so obvious, that in most of your pursuits, as well as almost everyone else, we are chasing after the rainbow with promises of happiness. Since childhood we have been exposed to beliefs about what should bring happiness.

Yes, the things we so desperately desire give us something to look forward to. And yet, once achieved, they no longer satisfy us with the pleasure we first experienced. Consequently, we are on a perpetual treadmill running towards superficial pleasures that gives us temporary happiness, because as you can see, they can easily be lost or taken from us.

Even the ancient Egyptian pharaohs believed that they could take material treasures with them to the afterlife, and were buried in ornate tombs surrounded by gold and silk. These desires for physical possessions are hypnotic and we automatically treasure them because we see others coveting the same things.

In realty, as Gurdjieff would say, this is an automatically robotic state and we are asleep. Our goal must be to awaken. Spinoza gives us that method of awakening our true intelligence.

The Awakening Process

What does the awakened state look like? In part 3, proposition 1 on page 130 of the *Ethics*, Spinoza explains, "That in certain cases the mind is active and in certain cases the mind is passive."

Active means when the mind's power of thinking is awake, and passive means that the mind is in a passive semi-conscious state or sleep state. All confusions, beliefs, reactions, and blindly chasing after desires express this semi-conscious state of being.

Active thinking is when the mind can see clearly and our ideas reflect the reality of nature. That is, we clearly see the objects before us, and when our mind is clear we see and act with confidence and understanding. With the application of reason, we can see the better path available for us and we follow what is tremendously helpful and beneficial to our and others' well-being.

In a passive state, we do not see very well, our vision is obscured and fragmented. I want to add that what is given to man are his five senses of touch, sight, hearing, smell, and taste. The body is bombarded with information it picks up through these five senses. Our sense of sight gives us an image of what we see, like a lens on a camera. The body is affected, modified by what it perceives, and the mind is likewise affected simultaneously, either painfully or pleasurably depending on our association with the object we perceive.

The active mind will process what the eyes see and endeavor to formulate ideas about what it perceives. Soon it begins to understand while reflecting upon its thoughts and deduces further truths.

The passive mind takes these images and puts in a limited effort toward understanding, and therefore only sees in a fragmented and confused manner.

For example, we see someone cutting into a long line at the DMV. We get upset and want to say something, but are too afraid to speak up. However, we feel pain, hate, and anger. This can only come about because we believe the individual has free will.

He is not supposed to do that," we think about the person who cut into line. "What he is doing is wrong."

You can see that we only have a fragmentary sense of reality. We cannot see the whole picture. We don't realize that this individual is following the law of necessity. It is necessary that he behave this way because he's following all the knowledge he has. His belief is that he can do whatever he feels like doing and he does not consider the feelings of others. He may have learned this behavior from the environment he grew up in.

An Active State

In a state where the mind sees and understands, our thoughts and ideas are clear and they reflect what we perceive, the reality of nature. This is a whole new state of being which develops over time as you apply your mind to problems. Your active awakened state will develop more and your mind and your whole being will become stronger and alive.

Facing everyday problems will be your opportunity to enlarge your being, that is, your understanding. The active mind loves to work and reflect upon its thinking in solving problems. It understands that in working on problems, it expands its effort and it is in the effort that it strengthens and enlarges itself. It lives in the world of reality, the magnificent present, the now. This active state expresses intuition and reason, which allows us see that we are a part of the whole of nature, that is, we are conscious of a connection with the divinity of nature.

Ego and Personality

The ego-personality state expresses itself when our mind is passive. Our thoughts and ideas are fragments, partial, and confused. We are unable to see the reality of things. The ego-personality lives in the imagination. It imagines it has free will and free choice.

As Spinoza explains on page 113 of his *Ethics*, this is the first and lowest level of knowledge. This is where the ego thrives, in the passive mind. It relies on memory and is past-minded and lives in an imaginary exaggerated world.

We are born into an ego state. It helps us survive and exist in life. The ego is a sense of self, but this self is not solid. It is like a shadow, It lives in the first and lowest level of knowledge, and its knowledge is comprised of hearsay information and by daily experiences that are not really understood.

As children we are told what is true and false, what is good, bad, right and wrong. We never question our authority figures, our parents, guardians, or our school system.

Society has an expectation of how you should behave. Society's laws are designed to keep its citizens obeying and following its laws, and to prevent them from causing harm to others. However, the ego is all we know. It follows the laws of necessity and self-preservation.

Gurdjieff explains on pages 161-63 of *In Search of the Miraculous* that personality is necessary. He says that it is the material, the source which an awakened intelligence can grow from, by studying our ego-personality nature.

In reality, we cannot willfully remove our ego and act from a higher level of consciousness or being. There is a process of learning how to study the personality-ego and see how it expresses itself through everyday activity. We must learn how to study ourselves without judging everything we see.

You will realize how difficult this is. If you judge what you are beginning to see as inadequate, stupid, and weak, then endeavor to acknowledge that you are judging yourself. Acknowledging that what we perceive needs improving is an intelligent process. There will be resistance, because the personality-ego is our dominant nature. It operates and reacts emotionally without thoughtfully examining the situation that triggers us. This is a painful feeling, and it reacts with hate and anger.

Spinoza on Perfection

It is important to understand what Spinoza means by perfection. Spinoza saw that reality and perfection are synonymous. So, coming to more perfection means coming to more clarity and reality. Pleasure is a state of greater perfection, while pain is a state expressing less perfection.

We are told and programmed early in our lives that man is not perfect, that only God is perfect. This is confusing because of our association with the word "perfection". Spinoza uses the words "perfection" and "reality" as the same thing.

More perfection, we live in more reality. Meaning that we are able to function, do our job, continue in whatever pursuits we desire. Less perfection, less reality. Meaning that our power to pursue what we want is inhibited.

For example, say you are following an instruction booklet while trying to connect new printer to your computer. Your knowledge of computers is extremely limited, and the directions do not make sense to you. You experience tension, stress, and anxiety. You do not know what to do. Pain, hate, and anger may follow.

However, if you make new efforts, in time things seem to go the way the instructions were intended and the printer now works. You experience pleasure, which is a feeling of power that we are able to perform the task before us. Therefore, more perfection and more reality, that is, the ability to accomplish the intended goal.

Improving Our Understanding

A very important method of improving our understanding appears on page 8 of Spinoza's *Ethics*:

"Having laid down these preliminary rules, recapitulating [summarizing, reviewing] all the modes of perception that are available; so that I may choose the best, and at the same time begin to know my own powers and the nature which I wish to perfect and improve."

So, we want to review and summarize the best mode (way) of perception that is available for us. There are four levels of perfection and I want to choose the best:

1. Such as by hearsay and,

2. By mere experiences that we have and do not question;

3. By seeing the essence of one thing is referred from another thing, which is a more exact way of seeing things; and lastly,

4. When the mind sees and understands the nature and the essence of the thing in itself – directly and without a need to compare, measure, or prove it to be true.

Spinoza examined and reflected upon what would be the best and most useful level of perception to achieve his end. What were his aim, goal, and purpose? On page 6

Spinoza explains that he wanted to come to "the knowledge of the union existing between the mind and the whole of nature."

What is he talking about? It is about coming to the knowledge of oneself, to identify specific emotions that are triggered, to know them specifically, and to see where we are mentally weak and confused, and to know when we are clear and understand. It is in this kind of effort we awaken the higher level of intelligence.

I want to emphasize that this is what Gurdjieff refers to as the fourth level of consciousness, an enlightened state of being. This clarity of mind will be directly connected with God's intelligence or the whole of Nature.

I also want to stress the importance of Spinoza's philosophy. He understood and saw both intuitively and clearly that God or Nature is comprised of infinite and eternal attributes; however, we are only a part of two, the infinite and eternal attributes of "Thought" and "Extension."

The attribute of "Thought" expresses the infinite understanding: when our ideas are clear, we understand and are in union with Nature's infinite understanding. We are thinking clearly and specifically. Without this attribute, the ability to think would not exist.

The attribute "Extension" expresses the physical universe. Our body is a mode that expresses this attribute and the attribute is modified many times; eventually, it is modified to a finite level of existence. All of God or Nature's attributes are infinite and eternal. We, however, are finite beings who exist for a limited period of time.

Boy on a Skateboard

Several years ago, I lived in San Pedro, California. I had a great ocean view apartment, and from my window I could see a young boy who lived in the neighborhood spend many hours each day applying great effort practicing tricks on his skateboard so that he could impress his friends.

Why did he do this? We always pursue what will bring praise and admiration for our skills and abilities. We constantly want approval and acceptance from our peers.

So, this boy practiced on his skateboard in order to be accepted. This is called ambition, in Spinoza's terms. It is the desire to do whatsoever in order to win approval and acceptance from our peers.

Skateboarding takes great effort requiring talent and physical abilities. It challenges the body's balance as well as mental and emotional patience. This is an example of what a teenager might do to belong, to be accepted and to make friends.

Likewise, we could apply that kind of effort to learn how to become a student by observing oneself objectively without judgments, for the sheer purpose of improving our understanding. We would achieve clarity, improved mental powers, increased self-confidence, and would be living by being in the reality of the now.

Unfortunately, human nature follows laws: The law of self-preservation, the law of necessity, the law of inertia, the law of cause and effect, and the law of following the path of the least resistance.

Obviously, all this is obscure to man. He does not know that his mind – his true intelligence – is asleep. He follows his desires, reactions, and instincts automatically and unconsciously.

Spinoza's Method

Now let's go to page 12 of the *Ethics*:

"So, in like manner the intellect by its native strength, makes for itself intellectual instruments, whereby it acquires strength for performing other intellectual operations, and from these operations receives fresh instruments, or the power of pushing its investigations further, and thus gradually proceeds till it reaches the summit of wisdom. That this is the path pursued by the understanding may be readily seen, when we understand the nature of the method for finding out the truth, and of the natural instruments so necessary for the construction of more complex instruments, and for the process of investigation."

This is how I interpret when Spinoza says, "So in like manner the intellect by its native strength." He means that within the mind there is an inner mental muscle that exists naturally, not a physical thing but a mental entity.

Spinoza begins to explain his method of investigation and the natural intelligent instruments of the mind. What is an instrument? An instrument to Spinoza is an idea, a thought in the mind, and that thought reflects something existing in nature. It is a mental affirmation expressing the mind's nature, so it necessarily knows intuitively what it understands, and it knows that it has a clear and true conception.

In other words, we know clearly and intuitively when we come across truth. We see and understand the nature of reality that our ideas reflect the reality of nature or existence.

In the final paragraph on page 12 of the "Improvement," Spinoza talks about the natural instruments so necessary and that are supplied by nature. Nature has provided for all of its subjects, all species of animal, including human nature with its five senses: touch, sight, hearing, smell, and taste. From these five senses we learn how to navigate the world around us.

Nature provided natural tools for primitive man: a fish bone to cut with, a rock to throw and bring down game, a tree branch to spear with, etc. He learned by trial and error how to survive, to swim, to fish, to forage for food, and to use a leaf to drink water. Eventually, man's mind began to increase his powers to think, and he developed more complex tools over time. Eventually, he invented the spear, the bow and arrow, the importance of a community, and the art of growing crops.

As we continue through pages 12-14, Spinoza lays out a specific method of doing exactly that, improving our understanding. As you attempt to follow, you can see how difficult it is to try to study on your own. To understand these difficult ideas you must seek help from someone who has gone through the process of improving their own understanding.

I too had difficulty with this, and it has taken me years of dedicated study. Fortunately, my teacher, the late Gregory Grover, taught me how to be patient and over time my intuitive nature embraced reason to increase the powers of my mind to come to ideas and to think clearly. Hopefully with my help you too will come to understand how to apply Spinoza's method to improve your own understanding.

I repeat, we must acknowledge that there are two parts to our mind, the active and the passive. The active part wants to understand and loves making the effort to address and solve problems. The passive part of the mind relies on memory, and it imagines it already knows everything. This is where our ego was born and resides. It believes in free will and desires to put the least amount of effort toward whatever problem comes its way. The passive mind procrastinates and wants to avoid problems.

You can see how difficult it is to understand the *Ethics* on your own. I want to acknowledge in you a desire to increase your understanding so that you may realize the possibility of coming to a new character that is different from your natural ego state of being. You are becoming aware of how challenging it is to understand the material before you, but fortunately I am here to help you go through these most difficult ideas step by step.

You may think that you do not need assistance. That is okay. Put in some effort and see how far you get. Unfortunately, many people who try this end up putting the *Ethics* on the shelf to collect dust. I want to emphasize here that this book serves to improve your understanding, and through reason and intuition it will change and increase the power of your being. Then you may come to the character that Spinoza saw as a goal.

He saw a deep connection in the knowledge of a union existing between his mind and the whole of nature. This knowledge is a knowing of oneself, and knowing the nature of God or Nature, and in this knowing we experience a direct connection and communication with this infinite and eternal being.

Consequently, joy, happiness, freedom from emotions, peace, and fulfillment follow.

My Own Growth

I too have been through the process of learning how to awaken my essential intelligence, the active thinking part of my mind that wants to understand.

Gurdjieff explains on page 161 of *In Search of the Miraculous* that there is a great difference between essence and personality. Essence is that which is our own. It is a process of knowing one's nature, the causes of our emotions and desires that direct our lives. This is a conscious effort, the effort to understand.

On the contrary, personality is that which is not our own. It is everything we learned since infancy, such as imitated and learned behavior. Personality which is an extension of our ego follows beliefs, attitudes, habits, and patterns of behavior. All this information is our collected knowledge and is stored in our brain as memory that helps us exist and function in life.

Man suffers because of his belief in free will and his knowledge is fragmentary and confused. Over time, we learn that the ego is our passive thinking mind and the goal is to activate the creative thinking part of the mind.

Therefore, my plan is to help you learn to see that the awakened state of the mind will increase its powers of understanding, and in this effort you will learn to understand your emotions. Your emotions are a key to freedom.

As I take you directly to the *Ethics*, as you learn Spinoza's language you will begin to connect his knowledge with your nature. This process will help you improve your understanding.

The Emotions

I must stress the significance and importance of understanding part three of the *Ethics*, "On the Origin and Nature of the Emotions."

On page 128, Spinoza wants us to understand that man is governed by cosmic laws, such as the law of necessity and the law of self-preservation. These laws direct man to act and express his being not from free will or free choice, but that he necessarily follows from what he understands. And if his understanding is confused, he will act in a confused manner. We are ignorant of the forces of nature, the natural causes that direct our desires and emotions.

Spinoza goes on to say, "Most writers on the emotions and on human conduct seem to be treating of matters outside nature rather than of natural phenomena following nature's general laws. They appear to conceive man to be situated in nature as a kingdom within a kingdom. For, they believe that he disturbs rather than follows nature's order, that he has absolute control over his actions, and that he is determined solely by himself."

As you will begin to see, Spinoza is endeavoring to help us realize that in reality, we are following unconsciously laws that express nature, and we are subjected to those laws.

On page 129, Spinoza explains how these laws of nature work and he says some things that are unimaginable even today, and that psychotherapy still has no clue of.

"Thus the passions of hatred, anger, envy, and so on, considered in themselves, follow from the same necessity and efficacy or power of nature; they answer to certain definite causes, through which they are understood, and possess certain properties as worthy of being known as the properties of anything else, whereof the contemplation in itself affords us delight."

Spinoza is telling us that once our mind is actively thinking, that in time, we will observe our emotions with wonder. A joy of seeing and reflecting upon the flaws or weaknesses without judgment, and in seeing ourselves we begin to gain a deeper and stronger sense of self, and the real 'I' of intelligence will manifest.

We must learn how to discern the difference between the awakened intelligence and the ego-personality, which is in a semi-conscious state and is the normal place we live. This increased power of mind increases a sense of 'I' and it is a new Intelligent self that we want to come to and to understand.

That is why we feel so good about ourselves when we learn to enjoy and love our efforts and the desire to understand. We will feel increased mental powers and feelings of fulfillment during this process. Extra effort is necessary to understand; actually, any amount of sincere effort stimulates our intelligence to think. In a way, you are extending your mental muscle; similarly, the body when it exercises its muscles expands and this is what we want to do: enlarge the mind, to stretch the mind.

Spinoza explains on page 130, definition number 3 at the top of the page, "By emotion, I mean the modification of the body whereby the active power of the said body is increased or diminished, aided, or constrained, and also the ideas of such modifications."

What does Spinoza mean by an emotion? What does it mean to be modified? These are both excellent questions and let's see if I can help you grasp this reality.

By emotions, I mean the body is being modified. It means we are affected, and there is a change in the body. We may feel pleasure or pain because of the object we are looking at. Pleasure is an increase of power and pain is a decrease of power.

This material is amazing in its potential to help us understand the nature of our emotions and to free us from being overwhelmed by them.

Dolores Case Study

My student Dolores came to me in May 2019 after reading about Gurdjieff and Spinoza. She wanted to develop a better sense of self and not be so needy and dependent on men. She is very intuitive and insightful and thought that I could help her increase her ability to focus and think clearly.

Here is an experience she had with her boyfriend Joe.

Dolores was worried that her boyfriend of eight months was seeing another woman. She observed Joe responding to a text message while they were dining. Dolores was modified – affected in a painful way – when Joe replied to the text he had received. She felt pain, a decrease of power. Being modified means that there is a change in the body and mind simultaneously. Dolores was affected in a negative way and realized that he was seeing another woman and got up and left him.

The way I work is to lead students to learn how to face their emotions, to be with them and to feel them. We must begin to discern the difference between the ego-intellect and our essential intelligence. This process is to awaken our intelligence that desires to understand.

I also believe that journaling about the events that trigger our emotions is extremely helpful. It is an important part of awakening the intelligence. This process of self-observation must be done without judgments, and this effort activates and awakens our intelligence as we desire to understand.

This is the more advanced part of the mind, the intelligent rational thinking mind. It works with reason and intuition. Spinoza explains the importance and the nature of the understanding, and in time the student will begin to learn and taste his or her intelligence that endeavors to understand. The student will know the difference between the understanding and the ego-intellect.

The understanding gives us feeling of well-being, a sense of fulfillment as we improve upon it. This understanding expresses the essential intelligence: its main interest is to be and live in reality. It knows that it understands, and it endeavors to improve itself. It is never static; it is a continuum.

Like an oak seed when planted, properly watered, receiving sunlight and all the necessary nourishment. Its nature is allowed to grow and it eventually becomes a giant oak tree.

We start this work with a childlike level of understanding. It grows with life's challenges and the difficulties we face, and with effort that growth and power will be self-evident.

Spinoza on Active and Passive Mind

Let us review the *Ethics*, proposition 1 on page 130.

"Our mind is in certain cases active, and in certain cases passive. In so far as it has adequate ideas it is necessarily active, and in so far as it has inadequate ideas, it is necessarily passive."

Proof: "In every human mind there are some adequate ideas, and some ideas that are fragmentary and confused. Those ideas which are adequate in the mind are adequate also in God since He constitutes the essence of the mind."

Spinoza is explaining that an active mind is thinking clearly, it knows what it knows.

For example, as a seven-year-old learning simple math I struggled with multiplication. I could not understand that 4 x 4 = 16. I was aware that my classmates could grasp this concept, and after struggling and applying mental effort towards the multiplication problem, a light in my mind saw clearly.

"Yes, now I understand."

This is thinking clearly. The light in our mind sees the truth. That is what I am talking about. We really do not understand the importance of learning. We grew up in the world of comparison and competition. The school system is not concerned with who or what you really are. You are basically a number in the classroom. Each child represents the school being financially compensated for the number of students in attendance.

God and the Mind

There are two words here that must be clarified, "Constitute" and "Essence".

By constitute we mean "make up," and the word essence expresses its nature, the idea of something. You may already have an intuitive feeling about this now. In time you will know more, trust me.

This is the place to talk about intuition. Spinoza explains that the highest level of knowledge is intuition. The irony is that we must have intuition to grasp this!

Intuition is seeing and knowing the nature and the essence of a thing. For example, consider a smartphone. It is a physical object. It has a shape, size, and weight, and is comprised of components with hundreds of tiny parts. It is like a computer, with circuit breaker, RAM, keyboard, microchips, etc.

But what is the essence, the nature, and the idea of a smartphone? The essence and the idea are communication. This may seem difficult, however, in time you will grasp it. In the process of learning this new language, a new way to stimulate the mind, you must ask a question without judgment.

"How can I better understand this?"

Be curious. Ask open questions. Eventually, ideas will come to you. This is the nature of the mind.

Desire is the Essence of Man

Desire expresses our nature, its essence. As long as we exist, we are always in a state of desire to preserve and maintain our existence. Consequently, we will do whatever is necessary to continue to persist in our existence.

The strength or weakness of how we persist depends on our knowledge. If our knowledge is confused, then our power of thinking is weak and we see in a confused way. When we do not see reality clearly, it is like wearing a pair of broken glasses and making it almost impossible to see.

We also imagine and believe that we and others live from free will and free choice. For example, you may judge someone for acting irrationally or scream at someone for being too slow in the checkout line when you are in a hurry. This is automatic; you have no choice but to react. You really do not see nor understand the problem of what is going on.

We only see a small part of reality, and do so superficially. Consequently, desire necessarily manifests and expresses our nature. We want this, we want that, we desire to go here, go there, and go everywhere. Desires express our whole being. If we achieve what we want or our if our desires are met, we feel pleasure. If our desire is not satisfied, we feel pain.

Meaningful Relationships

Being eighty years old, I have a relationship that I thought that I could have only dreamed about. In fact, I could have never dreamed of such a connection and love that I have with Margaret.

Margaret is from New York, highly educated, a successful businesswoman in the wine and spirits industry. She retired from that business and became a teacher in New York City. She has raised two boys who are now in their mid-thirties, and previously took care of her father as he got older.

Eventually she moved to Santa Monica, California. We met in the parking area of our senior living apartment complex. I had never thought of looking for or having a relationship. When I saw this attractive woman, I asked if she texted. She said yes. Then I asked if she would be interested taking a walk. She said yes.

Santa Monica is a beautiful city next to the Pacific Ocean. It has a popular pier with a roller coaster, Ferris wheel, lots of restaurants, arcade games, and people displaying their musical talents. It can be quite busy with tourists that come from all parts of the world. It is fascinating to walk and hear all the different languages being spoken.

Margaret and I have been together five years as of June 1st, 2021.

From this example you may see the benefits of this work that I do. "What is the work?" you may wonder. It is coming to a new sense of self, the 'I' of understanding that is connecting with an awakening intelligence. Learning Spinoza's method through his philosophy and teachings.

Over the years, improving my understanding by examining my nature without judgments, I was able to see from the light of my mind's eye the truth of how I was being. By examining without judgments my thinking, beliefs, attitudes, premises, and habits.

I learned to discern the difference between my ego mind and my true essential intelligence. You may have heard of alchemy, which was alleged to be a process of turning lead into gold. This transition, going from our ego sleep state of being into an awakened intelligent active thinking state, is alchemy in its truest form.

In our ego state, we are ignorant of the causes of our desires and how they determine our existence. The ego lives from its emotions and instincts; consequently, life can be a mess. Most of us are judgmental, angry, living in fear of rejection and criticism. We're always wanting approval and worried of making mistakes and concerned of what other people think of us.

It has taken me many years to realize and live by this higher level of intelligence. My ego still expresses itself, but more importantly, I can see it and it doesn't dominate my life like it used to. Essentially, I live more and more each day with an active clear-thinking mind. However, I also experience confusion when I get lost in expectations that other people should behave differently. I have to remind myself that I and others do not have free will or free choice.

When I see and understand that we all follow from the laws of necessity and self-preservation, my mind shifts into a state of reality, of being in the present. It is truly amazing what this work has given me. I am truly happy and I would like to share this because I love the life that I am living.

Being in this work, I have developed a deeper sense of self, an active thinking mind through Spinoza's teachings and philosophy. My partner Margaret is amazed that at my age I constantly come up with creative ideas when facing life's daily challenges.

I am eternally grateful to my teacher, the late Mr. Gregory Grover. He helped me to learn the value and joy of understanding and the importance of putting in extra effort.

You too can improve your life and change it for the better. People will be attracted to you because of your focus and calm demeanor. Your vision and your ability to see reality will improve, and you will make better choices, because everything we do is toward preserving yourself at the highest level.

Letter to Students

The following is an excerpt from a letter I wrote to my students several years ago:

It is important to remember that understanding how to study oneself is a work in progress. As you continue to apply your mind in the effort to understand, and not just to get answers but to really understand, that is where the magic is. What is the magic? Awakening the mind and knowing the difference between itself and your memory.

You may find more clarity as you study chapter 7 of *How to Solve Life's Problems*, which is titled "Discriminating Between Your Intelligence and Memory."

We must see where you are and where you want to go. Knowing your emotions, their definition and their meaning, and learning how to surrender to the feelings they elicit. As you study the *Ethics* – particularly pages 3 to 44 of "On Improvement of the Understanding," and part three, "On the Origin and Nature of the Emotions," beginning on page 128 – it is so important to ask yourself, "How can I understand this more? What does this mean?"

Acknowledging that you don't understand something is important. As you know, the *Ethics* is terribly difficult, so while reading see what you can understand and see what is confusing. Realizing what you do know and what you do not know is a great place to be.

At times we feel stuck and discouraged. The application of effort and more efforts in conjunction with reason and intuition are your tools to express your awakened intelligence, so that its understandings towards a higher level of spiritual consciousness and being are in a constant state of improvement.

Remember, you came to me for a reason. Was it a desire to change, to grow spiritually, or to increase a sense of self? Maybe at first you were not so clear about what you wanted. However, you were dissatisfied with where you are and you wanted something deeper, more meaningful, having a bigger purpose in life.

As you continue the work you will realize that facing your own inertia, your procrastination, and your resistance will be one of many great challenges. You may have wonderful intentions, yet there is a part of your nature that desires to go towards what is familiar and easy which is a natural human passive tendency. We are influenced and directed by the law of following the path of least resistance, the law of necessity, and the law of self-preservation.

Eventually, as you discover your awakened intelligence, there will be a struggle to discern the difference between that and your lower nature, which is a confused ego state. Strengthening the mind by factualizing the events that trigger your emotions is going to be your lifesaver. Factualizing will help you see as you tap into your higher intelligence and know the difference between itself and your lower nature and how the ego-intellect is an automaton.

We learned since infancy from our parents and our environment patterns of behavior that we follow necessarily to preserve our existence. This is how we learned to survive. Eventually you will discover and realize that you follow the law of necessity and that there is no free will. The idea that we have no free will is extremely hard to grasp. We have learned to believe since infancy that free will exists.

This is the first and lowest level of knowledge, "Hearsay and Experience." At this level, we do not understand that our ideas are fragmentary and confused. Not having our desires met brings pain, and then we suffer in doubt and fear. The emotions such as desire, pleasure, and pain are the foundation of all other emotions such as fear, hope, ambition, envy, pride, hate, and anger.

Spinoza saw and lived a life of great passion for clarity and truth. He understood that reason with intuition would help him see and connect with the whole of Nature or God. What a blessing this is! Once you learn what Spinoza found, you too will be blessed.

However, you must want it desperately and pay the price with exceptional efforts. Yes, great efforts in learning the language, participating in meetings with your teacher, listening to your recorded meetings, journaling your life's experiences, being patient, and most importantly, you must trust your teacher and follow his lead.

I love working with you as you apply your mind to work, to understand your nature and the cosmic laws that influenced you.

Letter of Gratitude

This letter came from a student named Aaron. I believe his triumphs and struggles are representative of what many people striving to improve their understanding go through:

Thank you for everything you have done for me. Thank you for fathering my spiritual growth. I wanted to say thank you. I'm sorry I have been ghosting and non-responsive. I want you to know I never had one disparaging thought about you or ever had a doubt in my mind you saw the truth and are a highly developed being. I do not know why I have not been responsive as I have been struggling with staying connected with many people in my life.

The reason I stopped meeting is a mix of causes that clouded the underlying truth, my ego believed that doing it alone is better. I truly felt I was not respecting your time as I was not coming to class prepared or canceling class on short notice without consideration. I genuinely felt with my lack of commitment it was better to take a break.

Another side of me had the perspective I needed real life and the truth of my ego to take me back to the work. Also, by throwing myself out there to observe my being will be the best in order for me to able to have a true taste of my passivity.

I recognize that your true being lies in the thirty-plus years of being with your own being and mastering it day in and day out. I never forgot how you explained how it took you a little while to connect with Spinoza intuitively after leaving your teacher's group. This was because you had to live and let the lessons soak in and express through your daily life, then take the steps of self-observation and factualizing to develop the being of those living from their reason.

That is what I truly seek and am coming to terms with. It is not an overnight process. I felt okay stepping back for a while, because being alone will teach me about the true nature of myself without the ambition of pleasing a teacher.

I do feel an overall growth in my intuition; however, I can see my being led by reason has not developed much at all. The power of seeking a future good over a present is still very weak. If you are open to speaking with me, I would love to. If not, thank you for everything and I love you dearly.

Thanks, Your student and Friend

Aaron

Comments on Aaron's Letter

Aaron worked with me for approximately three years. He was eighteen years old when he started. He has made great progress, and I am so happy for his growth. However, more effort is necessary to improve his understanding. Every individual who comes to this work is challenged to apply themselves to awaken the mind and comprehend Spinoza's methods for the improvement of one's understanding.

However, the ego state is very important and a major part of us. It dominates our nature and it imagines its powers and desires. We need the ego to learn how to survive and exist in life. Our ego state is a shadow of who we really are. It lives in the world of imagination and the lowest level of knowledge: hearsay and experiences. It acquires knowledge through the five senses and judges what is right and wrong by its limited perception. The ego lives in the world of emotions, such as, fear, hate, anger, envy, jealousy, pride, etc. It believes it has free will and free choice.

Gurdjieff explains that the ego and personality are necessary for inner growth. We must learn and understand how to study the nature of the ego without judgment.

Spinoza's method teaches us how to awaken our true intelligence so that we can begin to see and understand the difference between itself and our egoist intellect that relies on memory.

Attraction to the Work

Unfortunately, there will be only a few courageous individuals who are looking for something beyond the comfortable. Most people are tantalized by the ordinary objects of pursuit that occupy them, such as fame, wealth, and the pleasures of the senses.

At first, it may not be clear for the seeker what exactly it is that they are looking for. Gurdjieff expresses a reality that few are aware of, that man lives in a semi-conscious sleep state. He is implying that we all follow our desires unconsciously; we are driven and taken by them. We have many desires, such as for sex, food, entertainment, for a family, for wealth, fame, etc. All are good in themselves when taken in moderation. However, man often becomes obsessed, and then we cannot think of anything else but satisfying these desires.

Spinoza has given us a method of awakening our mind by exercising our intelligence to improve our understanding, so that in time we are able to moderate our desires and not be taken by them.

One thing is certain about this work, that in the beginning most people do not like where they are in life. Gurdjieff makes it clear that the individual must be dissatisfied. They are not happy, their life has no real meaning, and they feel intuitively that there must be something more.

My students usually find me through my website, videos on YouTube, or a recommendation by another student. My foremost desire is that a student will embrace Spinoza's philosophy deeply, to integrate, digest, and live his ideas. In time, the student must begin to awaken the mind and differentiate between itself and his old, conditioned memory. When our mind is clear we see and live in the reality of the now, the present.

One of the great obstacles for growth is the belief in free will. You too will be taken aback as you read this. You may ask, "What do you mean we do not have free will or free choice?"

Please bear with me. You will learn more as you continue reading and studying this book. Believing in free will is a belief and nothing else. It is handed down from generation to generation. We imitate and follow what our parents do, learning as children about how to exist in life. You were never taught how to reflect or study and ask questions about what you were told. We lack knowledge and understanding in examining oneself. Consequently, we automatically judge ourselves and others and complain about the world. There is an old saying, "We have found the enemy and the enemy is us."

Over the years, I have had the privilege of working with many people. Some stayed for a month, others for several years. My hope and desire is that what I communicate will have an impact on the individual. To help them see that they have within them an essential intelligence that can be awakened. Once awakened, the work on oneself really begins. We begin to learn the value of journaling by writing about the events and the situations that disturb us. There are specific emotions that we will express frequently, automatically, and in sequence when our desires are not met or satisfied.

New people endeavor to contact me after being introduced to my website, videos on YouTube, or from Facebook. They express an interest in Gurdjieff or Spinoza's ideas and teachings. I will invite them for a brief thirty-minute discussion about how I work. Many of these individuals live in other countries, so we communicate via Zoom, Skype, Google Invite, or WhatsApp.

Again, the method that I teach is to awaken our true intelligence. This intelligence expresses reason and intuition; it lives in the dynamic now. The difficulty is that we all come from an environment that influences us and conditions our nature. We follow rules, beliefs, and patterns of behavior that direct us in learning how to exist the best we can. Some naturally do better than others; however, this is a sleep state of being or a semi-conscious state.

Over a period of years, when the student has grasped and internalized Spinoza's ideas, it may be time for the student to go on his or her own and teach the ideas of Spinoza and Gurdjieff to others. I encourage this. I love to see these philosophers' ideas shared with those who want to awaken to a deeper level of reality and being.

There is an old proverb that says, "You cannot put a lamplight under a bushel." Likewise, the awakened mind is the light, and the light of your understanding and this wisdom must be shared.

A Former Student

One of my former students, Mike Turner, worked with me for over three years before deciding to go off on his own to communicate about Spinoza and other philosophers. Mike speaks in more general terms and covers a variety of different aspects of human nature. He is entertaining and has a growing audience on YouTube, but prefers not to communicate with people on a one-on-one basis because it takes too much time and effort.

Mike Turner has a fantastic photographic and auditory memory. While studying with me, he wanted to grasp Spinoza through his intellect without really understanding what he read. Mike is able to store lots of information in his memory and can recall that information and recite them word for word.

Gurdjieff talks about the different centers that we live by and explains that there is a great difference between knowledge and being. Knowledge without being becomes abstract and doesn't really improve or change our character. In other words, we cannot apply the knowledge. Gurdjieff explains that man has three centers: intellectual, emotional, and physical. However, one is usually dominant in each of us.

I recognized that Mike Turner favored his intellectual center. He studied Gurdjieff for over forty years, twenty on his own and the rest in Gurdjieff groups in across the United States and Europe.

One day, Mike was sad, depressed, and reminiscing about Gurdjieff. While browsing YouTube, he came across one of my videos and commented that I did not look like I was trying to cheat, demand, or persuade anyone. He said that I looked rather simple, honest, and had something interesting to say.

Mike had owned a copy of Spinoza's *Ethics* for ten years but did not understand its message. I began working with Mike, and his desire to learn was stimulated as he took hold of what I was communicating. His depression fell away as he took a new interest in a deeper study of his nature by applying Spinoza's ideas.

Being highly intellectual, Mike saw Spinoza as a challenge, and he took on the challenge as if it were a rabbit hole he had to explore to the very end. What he discovered, however, was that Spinoza had thousands of rabbit holes that needed to be figured out. Unfortunately, it is impossible to understand Spinoza's language in such a way.

What allowed Mike to break through and open up to Spinoza was accepting that he needed help. An important key was that he had an insatiable hunger, a desire to get what Spinoza was communicating. But first, he had to start facing his fears and anger. He had to learn how to factualize, writing in his journal about the events and situations that triggered his anger, hatred, and pain.

Spinoza explains that we live from the law of necessity and that it is necessary that we follow the knowledge we have. Consequently, man does not have free will because he cannot do anything other than what he knows or understands. This will always be a challenge to comprehend fully. For now, it is an abstract idea. We may repeat the words but to fully grasp it will take time. I have been doing this work for over forty years, and at times even I forget that I do not have free will, and I have to remind myself over and over again.

Remember, we do not choose to hate or be angry. It all falls under the law of necessity. It is necessary that you do whatsoever you do. I repeat, it is all automatic.

Mike went back into his memory and examined his childhood trauma. How did pain, hate, and anger manifest? What did he experience as a child? As we began to go deeper into his childhood, Mike acknowledged that he was psychologically and physically abused by both parents. He is one of four siblings, and when they talked, it was always about the abuse they took from their mom and dad.

I found this work utterly amazing; I continue to be in awe of it. There is an old medieval metaphor that said lead could be changed into gold through alchemy. We know that this is impossible, however we can still imagine and entertain the fantasy.

Fortunately, I see that this work is truly alchemical in its character: as we progress with great inner effort, this work literally begins to change our character from a sleep or semi-conscious egoistic state to an awakened intelligent conscious awake state of being.

Mike found that he had enough confidence and decided to create his own You Tube Channel. His audio recordings express a variety of thoughts and ideas relating to Spinoza, Schopenhauer, Buddha, Kant, and several other philosophers.

Mike has a great intellect, no question about it. He can absorb information and instantly recall it, but this is not enough. I emphasized to Mike that there is a great difference between gathering information and understanding that information.

Mike has attracted a good-size audience, however he does not work directly with individuals. Why? Because it requires time, great effort, and patience to go over these ideas step by step in hopes that something will begin to sink in and resonate in the minds of those interested.

As for myself, I will only work one on one with a student who is sincere. I am looking for the individual who is dissatisfied with their life and is searching for something meaningful. In the beginning, the individual may realize that he or she feels empty, fearful, lacking a sense of self, and desperately wanting approval. We must begin to see and look where we are without judgment, and with interest and the desire to improve.

Developing the Understanding

At the very beginning of the *Ethics* is the treatise "On the Improvement of the Understanding." This is an extremely important piece where we learn how the mind works and what the nature of an idea is. We are confronting a whole new language, learning the language of Spinoza. He explains his method of discerning what a true and clear idea is and how it differentiates between a false idea, fictitious idea, and the imagination.

Spinoza explains that a true idea is innate in us; the mind knows when it is clear and has a true idea. He also differentiates between the different levels of perception. We see and gather information through hearsay and mere experiences. This information becomes the first and lowest level of knowledge.

Perception arising from one thing is inferred from another, and this is how we get ideas from objects and then those ideas develop new ideas, etc. This is reason and is the second level of knowledge.

Lastly, there is perception which arises from seeing the nature and the essence of the thing directly without going through any process; we know that we know. This is intuition, the third and highest level of knowledge.

One thing which I have learned and hold to be true is that without embracing and understanding this part of the

Ethics, real spiritual growth is impossible. Therefore, a teacher is so necessary to take you on this exciting adventure, a journey of discovering how to understand with your mind and your heart.

You want to see, feel, and surrender with your whole being to the ideas that Spinoza conveys in his *Ethics*. Hopefully, in time you will experience the power of thinking. You must intuit that it is possible that you too can come to true ideas. But it takes work and I repeat, you cannot do this on your own. You may try and imagine that you are making progress; unfortunately, it is so easy to lie to ourselves and believe that we are making progress. Who are you testing your ideas with? You must have a teacher who is also a coach and a mentor to help you see your inner world.

Gurdjieff explained that our ego-personality is the material, the resource for our essential intelligent nature to grow from. For example, we believe in free will, and that approval comes from outside of us. We believe that love is to be won and that hate and anger are bad emotions that should be avoided. We must have a deeper aim, a purpose striving for something more meaningful that is potentially fulfilling.

This is what Spinoza realized. He wanted to come to a new character. His aim and goal was to come to the knowledge of the union that existed between his mind and the whole of nature. This knowledge first is to know oneself, our strengths and weaknesses, our emotions, and the process of strengthening the mind to see and understand clearly.

As our mind is strengthened, we begin to understand how this being called God expresses its nature through laws manifested in human nature. It takes time to understand the ideas and the language of Spinoza and Gurdjieff.

Gregory Grover

My late teacher, Mr. Gregory Grover, attracted hundreds of students. As students, we may have a desire for something meaningful and purposeful, and there are other desires that we have, such as wanting a relationship, fame, fortune, and being successful in life.

All existential desires compete with our essential desires. The first must satisfy the ego's desires, while the latter has to do with nourishing our true intelligence through journaling, factualizing, studying, and working with a teacher. The desire for growth through reason and intuition must be stronger than anything else. You must want this work desperately, as if your whole life depended on it.

As I reflect, I realize how much I love Spinoza's philosophy and how it literally has changed and improved my life. Eventually, when leaving my teacher's group after twenty-four years, I decided that I too wanted to start a study and work group to share what I had learned and how I had benefited from this work.

Gurdjieff had an excellent insight about human nature. He explains that the being of the individual is asleep and lives a life that is automatic and in a robotic state. Spinoza explains that we all live from our senses and instincts and follow from the lowest level of knowledge, which consists of hearsay and experience.

This is the first and lowest level of knowledge. The environment we grew up in was our original source of knowledge about life and the world. Our parents were our teachers: consequently, our knowledge is fragmentary, partial, and confused. We do not really see the truth or the reality of life. It is as though we see life through broken, distorted lenses.

All levels of suffering are manifested from the first level of knowledge. At this low level, we are led by our feelings, emotions, instincts, and imagination, which are all determined by our desires. Freedom from emotions can be achieved by understanding them.

Emotions are triggered and are necessary. They express our reactions to situations and circumstances that reveal to us just how confused we are, and how well we see reality. Fortunately, our emotions can be understood, and we can become free of them as we apply effort to understand them clearly and distinctly.

Susan Compares Buddhism to Spinoza

Susan found me through Facebook. In prior years she had studied Buddhism and was a dedicated follower, however she felt something was missing. After meeting with me she said that Spinoza's ideas really resonated with her.

Buddhism promotes the idea that we must suppress and avoid our desires. However, the idea is that desires are where our problems come from. If you think about it, there are temples, sanctuaries, and religious retreats where Buddhists practice and worship. They are isolated and immersed in meditation and other disciplines. If you go on a meditation retreat for two weeks, you will undoubtedly feel renewed, regenerated, and cleansed physically, mentally, and spiritually.

It is all wonderful, but as you return to your normal life, you will begin to feel the same emotions of desire, pain, hate, and anger as before. We all are easily triggered by what we see others doing that we disapprove of. We live in the world of should and should not, right and wrong, good and bad.

The basic problem is that we believe in the world of free will and free choice. It is difficult to comprehend that Spinoza understood that man lives by the laws of self-preservation and necessity. We do not understand because our mind is cluttered with erroneous information.

So, the Buddhists say, do not follow your desires, do not listen to them, because they are bad for you. I have worked with several students who previously practiced Buddhism and they shared with me how they found limitations in its teachings.

Spinoza explains that "desire" is the essence of man. By essence we mean the inner nature of man or the idea of man's nature. Everything that emanates from man's being, all of him, all his desire, wishes, beliefs, attitudes, clarity, confusions, love, hate, successes, and failures express his being.

However, the basic desire is to do whatsoever to continue to do the things that it believes are good. For example, I am hungry, I desire food. I desire to go on vacation. I desire to buy a new car. I desire to go to college. I desire to get married. I desire love. I desire people to approve of me. I desire to rob a bank. I desire sex.

Desire expresses the basic requirement of man, to preserve one's existence that follows from the law of self-preservation. It is our basic motivation to exist and persist to exist. In other words, you cannot live without desire. It is a part of our DNA, it is in you by the law of nature and you have no choice.

Therefore, the religious belief that you can remove your basic desires is impossible. As long as you are alive, desires must be expressed and communicate themselves.

Easter Sunday

I sent this message to my current and past students in order to express the true spirit of Easter:

Spinoza's ideas of God and Jesus are totally contrary to tradition, dogma, and formal beliefs. Spinoza was born a Jew. He was told that Jews were the chosen people and they believed in a personal God.

Spinoza broke free from this dogma and tradition. His idea of God being non-conventional was called heretical and atheistic. And yet, God is communicated throughout his *Ethics*. This work communicates a method of awakening the mind's intelligence, where reason and intuition are keys to expressing this intelligence.

Unfortunately, human nature depends on hearsay, beliefs, and the images of nature. People resist the effort to learn how to apply themselves deeply to understand. If you seek answers, you must have a question. How clear are your questions? What are you seeking? Truth, clarity, and understanding are available, but you must want them desperately.

The spirit of mankind is the mind, our intelligence. If the mind is clear and alive, it expresses wisdom and knows that we are a part of God's nature, and we are partakers of His divinity. The spirit of Easter is a rebirth of an awakened mind, the light of our intelligence.

Mankind, unfortunately, lives in a deep sleep and is unaware of the mind's potential. Believing in free will and free choice keeps mankind in shackles of despair and suffering. The awakened mind faces the difficulties of life and applies reason and intuition, always doing its best to find solutions to problems.

The Spirit of Jesus

Spinoza's idea of Jesus was as a man who had great wisdom about human nature, as well as Nature or God's infinite and eternal Being. Unfortunately, mankind is confused about what God actually is and believes that God made all things for man so man could worship Him. Consequently, traditional practices became a part of man's worship.

Spinoza explained the difference between Moses' and Jesus' understanding of the Nature of God. Moses experienced God through his body, emotions, and feelings. Moses heard a great voice; however, this can be easily misinterpreted.

The Ten Commandments were a manifestation of his interaction with this voice. Therefore, the Ten Commandments became religious law as rules on how to conduct oneself. It endeavored to create a societal order for the Jewish people. But it did not really help mankind understand his nature and the nature of God.

Spinoza understood that Jesus had communicated directly with God, mind to mind, as a living conscious connection with this infinite and eternal Being called Nature or God. He directly communicated with this Being's infinite and eternal intelligence which could be only understood intuitively.

In Spinoza's *Ethics*, it is all about coming to a new intelligent character, the higher mind of man, by improvement of its understanding. Consequently, we can come to know this Being's nature directly. However, first we must come to know oneself, to know our strengths and weaknesses and how well we see reality. We must increase our efforts to improve the powers of our understanding to see and know Spinoza's God: a Being with infinite and eternal attributes, the attribute of "Thought" and the attribute of "Extension," and where we are a mode of these two attributes.

Clear and true ideas express this attribute "Thought." In other words, we are a part of this Being's intelligence. Spinoza explains that God constitutes the essence of our mind. In this connection there is a union with this magnificent Being's mind.

However, man believes he has free will and is disconnected from this truth. Man believes he is the cause of his actions and his desires, but Gurdjieff explains that mankind is asleep to this reality on page 66 of *In Search of the Miraculous*.

Jesus endeavored to communicate to the masses via parables. When His disciple Peter asked why, Jesus in essence responded, "You can hear and understand my ideas. To those who do not understand, hopefully my parables will affect them if they can hear or see intuitively. If not, that is no bother."

Jesus and Barabbas

I watched and loved a movie called *Jesus of Nazareth*. It made a deep impression upon me, and I want to convey a spiritual idea that came to me afterward. You may not find this exact sequence of events in the Bible, but will see that the idea is important if taken intuitively.

In this story, Jesus is washing in the Temple's bathing area. He sees a man named Barabbas and thinks, "This man is intelligent, strong, and a leader of men. I wonder if he would be interested in what I do."

What was Jesus' purpose and desire? He wanted to share the idea that the Kingdom of God is within. What did he mean?

My interpretation is that God's Kingdom is within the clear, active awakened mind of man. When our ideas are clear we express a part of His intelligence and partake in His divinity.

Today, as through all of mankind's existence, he is lacking the knowledge of this intelligence, lacking in a higher conscious mind. He may not be able to see and understand this reality. Man believes that he is a kingdom within a kingdom. That he is separate from nature. That he is the cause of his desires and actions and believes in free will.

Barabbas had a small underground army who fought and killed the Romans. He looked at Jesus and thought, "This man attracts a lot of people, people trust him. I wonder if he would help our cause."

Barabbas spoke to Jesus as if Jesus was just another man. He could not see the depth of Jesus nor understand him, because Barabbas had no depth and lacked intuition. He was a man of existence only. Yes, he had an important cause, trying to free the Jews from the Romans.

Barabbas accepted Jesus' invitation to talk. Jesus spoke first, asking Barabbas if would he be interested in following His cause by saving the souls of humanity by awakening the mind and living from the Kingdom within.

Barabbas had no idea what Jesus was talking about, spoke angrily, and said, "We have a real serious problem here. People are dying and starving while being subjected to Roman domination. We are suffering, we must kill the Romans and free ourselves."

Jesus replied, "Those who use the sword shall die by the sword."

Barabbas walked away in disgust.

This is a classic example of how when the student is not ready, he cannot see nor hear the truth. Truth? What is the truth?

In Jesus' parables, there lies clarity in understanding the laws that govern and influence human nature and awaken the mind that expresses the truth within him. The heavenly state, or the kingdom within, is what Spinoza communicates in his *Ethics*. Coming to such a character, which is the knowledge of the union existing between the mind and the whole of nature.

This is the end and the aim that Spinoza wanted, living by it and wanting to share his wisdom to all who are interested. To understand the knowledge that is in Spinoza's *Ethics*, there is a method of awakening our intelligence and strengthening its understanding so that we can know the nature of God, this infinite Being's essence, and become conscious partakers of it.

This is truly a blessed and fulfilled and happy state of being.

Jack Case Study

Jack is is almost seventy years old and very unhappy. He feels that he always wanted to be someone other than himself. He feels uncomfortable in his own skin, and has feelings of not being good enough while always seeking approval from others.

I asked him if there was a situation which had triggered this desire for approval. He talked about a neighbor named Brian who is a police officer. Whenever

Jack goes out for a walk and passes Brian's house, Brian invites him over for a chat. Jack resists because Brian always brags about his successes. He is going to retire soon with a police pension, has made profitable investments, and plans to travel around the country in a new motor home.

Jack wished that he could just walk away without hurting Brian's feelings. He is afraid to express what he really wants, which is not having to endure Brian's bragging. However, Jack could not see a way out.

Gurdjieff explains that this is called external considering. We give priority to how other people feel over our own feelings. We are people pleasers and follow the wishes of others.

Spinoza reveals that there is even more going on. In prop 30 in part three of the *Ethics*, he explains that this is a state of ambition. Ambition is the desire to do what we see others doing, and we do so wholly to please them and get their approval. We observe what they are interested in and then express that we have the same interest in order to win them over.

We are seeking friends and will do whatever is needed to get them to like us. This is a passive state of being. We are all groomed into this kind of thinking, where power comes from believing that we are the cause of another person's pleasure or pain. In Jack's case, he is concerned about what other people are doing in order to show what a good guy he is.

Society is not interested in your inner life. You are a part of society, a worker, you pay taxes, learn a trade, make a living, raise a family, etc. Your mental health is ignored and dismissed. I think only recently have we become aware of the reality of mental problems.

My work with Jack has helped him see how to develop a sense of self by increasing the power of his mind through the process of factualizing and journaling the events and situations that disturb him. Our emotions are triggered in every situation, such as desire, pain, hate, and anger. These specific emotions will repeat themselves over and over when our desires are not fulfilled.

Jack studied his feelings and learned how to surrender to his pain, such as feelings of powerlessness, helplessness, and not knowing what to do. This process activated his mind, the intelligent thinking mind that wants to understand, which is wholly different from the passive mind that relies on memory and expresses the ego-intellect.

Spinoza explains in his *Ethics*, prop 1, part three, that in certain cases our mind is active and in other times it is passive. The active mind wants to understand, and it lives in present time, whereas the passive mind expresses confused thinking and is comprised of fragmentary information that is disconnected from reality.

Even though Jack is nearly seventy years old, he applies himself with a desperate need to understand his emotions when they are triggered. He attends weekly meetings, listens to a recording of our meeting, listens to other students' meetings, takes careful notes, and looks up the definitions of the emotions. In essence, he really wants to heal himself.

This level of effort and studentship in time will bring about a new sense of self that expresses a real intelligent mindset of thinking and problem solving. This process also develops feelings of self-approval, self-love, peace, happiness, and in time becoming in touch and connected with the whole of Nature.

Movie Ordinary People

The movie *Ordinary People* was released in 1985, and starred Donald Sutherland, Mary Tyler Moore, and Timothy Hutton. It exposes the problems of the lives of people, ordinary or not so ordinary. It reveals how in everyone's home, it is important and so necessary that we keep our little secrets, and put on a happy face of pretentiousness and superficiality.

We all learn exceedingly early from our parents and from others to hide the truth. We project an image of who we imagine we are, similar to wearing a mask. Another issue is that we complain about our problems while never learning how to study them, not only those involving our nature but most problems in life. We procrastinate or avoid facing problems. The truth is, we really do not know how.

That is why this work that I do is so significant and powerful. The awakened mind is at a higher level of consciousness. Similar to the idea of "awakening the light of the mind," it sees clearly and understands why we suffer. It knows why we are in pain and how to free ourselves from being overwhelmed by anger and hate.

I recommend the movie *Ordinary People* because it exposes the problems that are common in human nature. Most of us grew up in a family where the concern was how other people saw us or thought of us, and we always wanted to make a good impression, and not show weakness or mental problems. We learned to avoid anything that would cause shame, dishonor, and disrespect to the family. Your reputation was so important.

Since we were brought up to imagine that people are thinking about us, we constantly seek their approval as if it was the most important thing in the universe.

The benefit of this work is to identify the possibility of coming to a new character. This is embodied by knowing oneself through self-observation without judgments, learning how to extend mindful efforts to understand our emotions, as well as see our initial desire that was diminished, rejected, or not realized.

There is new activity in the mind that wants to understand and in this effort to understand, a new sense of self is born. The old self relies on memory and is a passive thinking thing. All our emotions are triggered when we live in this state.

Gurdjieff explains that "there is a difference between essence and personality." This quote can be found in an important section of Ouspensky's book *In Search of the Miraculous* on pages 161-163.

He goes on to say that essence is that which is our own, and personality is that which is not our own. Our own means that our own effort is to understand, and this understanding expresses our real intelligence that applies reason and intuition.

We can gain a higher level of knowledge and then we knowingly participate in the Divinity of His Nature. We love our mind's thinking and understanding. This state of being is where self-approval manifests.

That which is not our own is what we pick up, imitate, and copy by taking on others' attitudes, beliefs, and habits, all which are stored in our memory. We learn to talk, learn one or more languages, are educated how to exist and function in life. All of this is stored in our memory. Consequently, we never experience anything really new, but repeat old habits and live from old beliefs, resulting in feelings of desperation, emptiness, suffering, and pain.

However, innate in all of mankind there is a desperate need for happiness, self-approval, and self-love. The challenge is that we mimic our parents, just as they learned from their own parents how to be, and so on. Consequently, there is a mad scramble to find happiness and love outside our nature. We imagine the perfect man or woman, being married, having children, getting the perfect job, flashy car, living in a respected neighborhood, etc. Again, all this is not our own. We believe that the things everyone is chasing after will bring us happiness.

The mind is a thinking thing; it is a mode that expresses one of Nature's infinite and eternal attributes, the attribute of thought. Again, I will remind you, that the mind has two parts: in certain cases the mind is active and at times it is passive.

When we live from a passive thinking mind, we are not our own master. We become a victim of circumstances and we are easily influenced by the opinions of others. We live by the world of images, feelings, and imagination.

When it is active, the thinking mind wants to understand. It knows that the difficulties we encounter and the emotions we experience will be the food and the material for true spiritual growth. This leads to the improvement of our understanding based on clarity and truth.

When we apply our mind with the use of reason and intuition, this feeds the mind with the effort to understand.

Steve's Email

I recently received an email from Steve. He had originally contacted me after finding my website and was interested in discussing Spinoza. After several conversations, Steve wanted to know how did I arrive at and to come to such wisdom, and what makes me sure that I know the truth. He also asked how I learned to understand Spinoza's philosophy. Steve was brought up in a Christian teaching environment, and asked me how faith and belief fit in with Spinoza.

Here is my response to his email:

You were brought up in a Christian environment where faith and belief were important. However, do you feel that faith and belief are the way towards salvation? Are you uncertain and dissatisfied with where you are?

Obviously, you may be seeking answers, because you told me that you have studied Spinoza for over ten years and Gurdjieff much longer. Yet, how well do you understand what you read. This is why a personal teacher who has gone through the process of mastering Spinoza and Gurdjieff's ideas could help you see your nature without judgments, but objectively. Examining your thoughts, ideas, emotions, and feelings ultimately leads to freedom from them.

In part 5 of Spinoza's *Ethics*, propositions 2, 3, and 4 explain how to free ourselves from pain and suffering by separating our emotions from the thoughts of an external cause and focus on the emotions themselves.

For example, pain is a decrease of power, and anger is desire whereby through hatred we are induced to remove or destroy the object of our hate. Focusing on how the emotions work in us, what they are, their definition and their meaning, enables us to distance ourselves from the incidents that caused of our pain. This inner focus and the ideas that we come to regarding the specific emotions, creates a new sense of self, a new identity. This new sense of self expresses our greater intelligence, which is comprised of clarity through reason and intuition.

Normally we live in an ego-automatic-robotic state of being that depends on memory. It being the lowest level of knowledge, made up of hearsay and experience. We do not realize that our desires and reactions have previous causes that determine our nature. Thus unaware, we are driven by causes that express the law of self-preservation and the law of necessity.

It is by the law of necessity and not by free will that we do what we do, and this expresses the knowledge that we have. If you express anger and judgments in dealing with specific problems, this necessarily comes from a previous conditioning that we learned as a child.

When I asked, "Do you understand Spinoza's God?", you replied, "I don't agree with him." I am asking you again, do you really understand Spinoza's God?

In his essay "On the Improvement of Our Understanding," Spinoza shares a method of improving our mind to think clearly and true. He endeavored to take us on his path of discovering a purpose, an aim to fulfill our basic requirement and come to permanent happiness. He saw everyone chasing after fame, fortune, and the pleasures of our senses.

At one time he too had followed these pursuits, however, he realized they did not really provide the happiness he was seeking. He understood that chasing these basic desires was self-destructive and harmful because they would become excessive. It is impossible to moderate the desire for riches, fame, and sensual pleasures.

The "Improvement" gives us a foundation and a method of how to direct the mind to come to clear and true ideas. Spinoza points out that innate in the mind there is a knowing that it knows; that it can differentiate between falsity, fantasy, imagination, clear thinking, and truth.

Have you ever read the fifth part of the *Ethics*? Spinoza makes it very clear that reason by itself can only take us so far, and that to understand God or this infinite Being's nature and its attributes, intuition is necessary. Reason alone cannot take us there.

I want to make something clear. Some of us are born with different levels of intuition, just like there is a great range of intellectual competence. However, no matter what level your intuitive nature is, it must increase its development and growth. It is impossible to understand Spinoza's language from our original mindset, perspective, and attitude.

We must go through a change, a dramatic change of character. The obstacle is our ego identity. We are all born into an environment that stems from the first level of knowledge, which is hearsay and experience.

While Gurdjieff explains that man is asleep and must awaken, he does not really give us a clear path of how to awaken the active clear-thinking intelligence. Gurdjieff also emphasized that man cannot awaken by himself; he must have a teacher who has gone through the process of awakening.

It is so easy to lie to ourselves and imagine that we are making progress and growing spiritually. This is where Spinoza is so important; but again, to understand Spinoza you must also have a teacher that can help you understand his ideas, which are difficult. Otherwise it is impossible to grasp Spinoza's deep concepts by yourself.

If you are a highly intellectual type, you may have studied different philosophers, gone through different Gurdjieff groups, filled your mind with many thoughts and ideas that seem true and relevant. However, just as

Jesus, the man, said in a parable, "You cannot put new wine in old bottles," this must be grasped intuitively. New wine represents new and clear concepts. The old represents ideas we hold onto.

How can you take in what is so radically different from what you have always believed? It is impossible to grasp new concepts when you are filled with preconceived ideas and beliefs.

I was fortunate. I met my teacher, the late Gregory Grover, in 1970 and remained as a student for the next twenty-four years. He told me that he was not sure if this work was for me because my mind was very passive and weak, but eventually he saw something in me that I did not know I had, a deep intuitive nature.

I just knew that Mr. Grover had something special. Although I could not explain it at the time, I wanted what he had. He spoke with authority and clarity, and it affected me deeply. In time, I began to understand the nature of the mind according to Spinoza as my teacher had explained.

I must admit that I am a terribly slow learner. I must understand something with my whole being in order to "get" it. If an individual only applies intellectual effort, he cannot grasp intuitively the reality of Spinoza's ideas. I know Spinoza's philosophy is true and clear, but how do I know? I just know it. Can I explain it? Yes. Can you hear my ideas, my clarity? I doubt it.

You must go through the process, a transformation of living from your ego nature to discovering your true essential nature, an awakened intelligence that expresses the desire to understand.

Gurdjieff describes the idea of an awakened state to some degree on pages 161-164 in the book *In Search of the Miraculous*. In the middle of page 161 he discusses "Essence and Personality," where essence is that which is our own, and personality is that which is not our own.

The ego-personality becomes our identity, where we learn how to be, what to believe in, how to behave, talk, and walk from our parents and the environment we grew up in. This is not of our own making, it is all conditioning and learned behavior.

What is our own? Our deliberate efforts to understand our nature, our emotions, and our confusions. In other words, we own our clarity and the efforts of our understanding. This cannot be taken away from us.

Our ego-personality is necessary for our survival. We cannot willfully remove our personality and we cannot willfully change desires that are excessive or addictive. We must face the reality of our addictions and learn how to see what they are, what they mean, and what they give us.

A basic belief which is a great obstacle to true knowledge is the belief that we have free will. Do you ever questions this? There are over seven billion people on this planet, and everyone believes in it.

Spinoza's philosophy is based on clarity and truth and to know and understand the laws that manifest from Nature, or this infinite and eternal Being. If you participate in this work that I propose, in time you will be able to understand a few of these laws that govern and influence human nature and the whole of nature. These are the laws of self-preservation, necessity, cause and effect, inertia, and following the path of least resistance.

As a teacher, mentor, coach, and student of Spinoza and Gurdjieff's teachings, I take my students on a journey of how to look at oneself without judgment, which is difficult to do. We judge ourselves constantly, often experiencing shame and guilt. This is because we believe we freely choose to do the things that cause our problems. We don't realize that we are doing our best with the knowledge we have.

From the effort you make to understand this knowledge that Spinoza communicates, in time you will begin to see that there is a different way to be. Our emotions are most important because they tell a story, and we can discover how we are only perceiving and seeing things in a limited way. It's important to keep a journal where we write about the situations that triggered our emotions of pain and suffering.

Freedom from pain, hate, and anger comes about when we understand. Understanding is seeing clearly. Identifying specific emotions and understanding what they mean. Gurdjieff calls this information about our confused nature food for growth.

Spinoza's philosophy is exactly "ethics" in its nature. How to improve our understanding, how to learn to live by reason, and the necessity of intuition so we can come to the knowledge of the union existing between our mind and the whole of nature in which Spinoza came to as his purpose and aim.

Intuitively and with the aid of reason, I see that Spinoza has a key to improve our understanding, a method of awakening one's mind, the intelligent part of the mind that reflects upon it ideas that corresponds to the reality of nature. Spinoza, when understood, will give us the knowledge on how to improve our thinking.

I found and understand the truth that Spinoza communicates in his *Ethics*, and I so desperately want to share it. However, I accept that only a few will want to invest the time and effort necessary.

Mastering Oneself,

Lewis

Personal Story

In my own family of eleven siblings, our parents provided food, shelter, clothing, and all the other necessities. However, in the area of emotions and psychological behavior, it was a disaster. Our home was like a war zone filled with constant fighting and arguing. My parents would recite their favorite rants, like "Why are you so stupid?" and "You cannot do anything right."

Living in that environment, my brothers and sisters suffered terribly from a poor sense of self, feelings of failure, and inadequacy. Many turned to alcohol and drugs to lessen their pain. Two of my brothers could never participate normally in society or be productive because their fears of rejection and failure were overwhelming.

In my own life I lived with a feeling of fear about what people thought of me. I feared making mistakes or saying something stupid. And yet, I was still able to live a productive life, despite these feelings of deep inferiority that plagued me.

Over a period of time, my teacher Gregory Grover taught me how to improve my understanding, and how to increase my efforts to apply my mind toward problems. Eventually, I learned to embrace an intelligence I thought I never had.

This is an awakened and enlightened state of being.

Essay: "Discriminating Between Your Intelligence and Memory"

This essay was written by my late teacher, Gregory Grover:

Are you becoming aware that almost everything you do is based on responses of memory patterns to present problems, situations, circumstances, and the like? We are all programmed early in life with different patterns that become embedded in our memory banks. The result is that almost all of our mature existence has been predetermined, so that instead of living spontaneously in the now we are responding mindlessly – that is, without consciousness, to various external stimuli.

As a result of these deeply rooted patterns in our memory, we are under the illusion that we make choices out of free will. When you begin, dimly at first, to recognize the great difference between your intelligence and your memory, your intelligence will slowly and gradually become activated so that you will be able to begin responding to problems and circumstances by asking yourself real questions.

By asking yourself, "What do i think about this now?", you are not merely responding from preset patterns. You will consult your memory and use it as a tool, and then make decisions based on the best thinking you can do now. This consulting your intelligence will slowly strengthen it, and you will enter on the training path needed to discriminate between your dynamic intelligence and your passive memory. Then a process of growth will begin in your intelligence. In time you will discover yourself becoming more alive and you will experience a new kind of joy based, not on externally produced sensations, but on the inner sense that you are really on the path of true self-fulfillment.

My Comments on Memory and Intelligence

We encounter problems every day. However, we only make a limited effort when dealing with them, just enough to get by. By nature, we all want to avoid problems; yet problems inevitably arise. A plumbing issue, a flat tire, lost keys, losing a job, feeling lonely, fear of intimacy, fear of rejection, judging ourselves, and feelings of inferiority.

We depend on our memory to solve problems. Since childhood we were programmed with deeply set patterns about how to do things, how much effort we should apply to our problems and challenges. Consequently, we are predetermined to respond to every problem we face unconsciously, automatically, and with the lowest level of effort. However, we act necessarily, with the knowledge we have learned: there is no free will in these decisions.

Here, my teacher is introducing the idea that we possess an intelligence which is different from the passive part of the mind that relies on memory. When we become aware of this intelligence by learning how to face our nature through the process of factualizing our emotions of desire, pain, hate, and anger, then the mind is forced to apply itself to understand.

It is in the effort to understand that awakens this great intelligence within us. I want to emphasize that it takes deliberate effort going through this process over and over again to strengthen the mind. The mental muscle of the mind is meant to understand. There is a great difference following from the intelligence compared to following from memory. The intelligence is a dynamic living thing, while the memory is old and stagnant.

For example, have you ever seen a waterfall? It is powerful, dynamic, a living thing. You take a photo of it and the picture is nice, you frame it and hang it on the wall. You pass by it, you pause and feel pleasure, you recollect the feelings and emotions the waterfall elicited – but it is all in the past.

Are you living life in the present, in the now? The goal is to be aware of the difference and know when you are actively thinking.

Hugh Case Study

Hugh is seventy years old. He has difficulty connecting with Susan, his wife of thirty-five years. They have three adult children now raising families of their own. Hugh is retired, spends a lot of time with his wife, and is literally bored with his life. He complains that Susan watches stupid rom-coms all day. He has contempt for her inability to have intelligent conversations. She then accuses Hugh of being distant, aloof, and without any feelings or compassion.

Hugh found me through watching one of my videos and visited my website. He felt that something was missing in his character and wanted to change. Overall he did not feel whole and was unhappy. He told me that he avoided emotions and was afraid of them because they are so unpredictable. In turn, he avoided any kind of confrontation.

Hugh was previously involved with a Gurdjieff work and study group for over fifteen years, where it was encouraged that one should not express negative emotions. He favors his intellectual powers, and the way I work with a student is to help them see and realize that they have a higher-level state of consciousness. This is an awakened clear mind that wants to improve its understanding through the problems that affect us, that trigger our emotions, such as desire, pain, hate, and anger. There are many more emotions. However, these four are the ones we will focus on.

Here is an example from Hugh's life:

Hugh was standing in line at a grocery checkout, and he was wearing his mask while social distancing. A young woman was holding her child a foot away, and he could feel her breathe. He was paralyzed and afraid of confronting her by saying, "You are too close, please keep your distance."

He was afraid of upsetting her, imagining the worst-case scenario of causing an emotional outburst. Hugh's desire was to be safe and distance himself from others, but he believed that his space was being violated. He felt pain, hate, and anger. Anger was Hugh's desire to remove his pain, and hate was his belief that the young lady was the cause.

I suggested we go directly to the pain, feelings of powerlessness, helplessness, and not knowing what to do. As Hugh took the time to review the situation that triggered his emotions, this began to stimulate his mind, and it became activated. Once his intelligence was awakened, it wanted to understand the problem.

Self-reflection without judgments forces the mind to consider new ideas, and this is where we get our power: the desire to understand. An intellectual person must learn to embrace and surrender to their feelings and emotions. Feel the pain of helplessness and powerlessness and stay with it. Don't run from it.

In time, Hugh will learn to go deeper and learn to feel. This is what he wants because he knows that this will make him more conscious and fulfilled.

Paul Case Study

My student Paul told me about a situation that triggered his pain, hate, and anger. One night he decided that it would be better to wash the dishes after dinner rather than let them pile up. While he was standing at the sink, his wife Cathy came up and told him he was using too much soap.

He said, "Okay."

When he began to use a scrubbing tool his wife said that it is not used for pots and pans. Paul got fed up with Cathy constantly trying to correct him.

"You do the dishes then," he said and walked away.

This was an expression of frustration, pain, hate, and anger because Paul believed that Cathy has free will, and that she was freely rejecting Paul. He wasn't thinking about how Cathy has her own ideas about how things are done.

These types of situations are nature's way of challenging us. Either we react or we endeavor to understand the emotions that follow from what we perceive as an offense. In Paul's mind, he always wants to be approved of and fears rejection. He believed that Cathy was rejecting his efforts at washing the dishes.

As Paul began to factualize in his journal he started to see his feelings of powerlessness, impotence, helplessness, and not knowing what to do. These are basic feelings that most people avoid. Anger is our way of wanting to remove the pain we feel and the desire to get our power back. However, we never get to the root of the problem this way.

In surrendering to our feelings and emotions, this opens the gateway to the active mind that wants to understand. The active mind is an awakened state, it is the light of the mind. It lives in the moment and desires to put in the effort to understand. To comprehend this process, intuition plus reason is required.

Fortunately, over time and with repeated efforts in endeavoring to understand, Paul is beginning to see and comprehends that effort is power that expresses his understanding.

Matt Case Study

Matt began to study with me after watching my videos and reading through my website. He was aware of Gurdjieff and Spinoza but had never studied them before. He is highly intellectual and avoids his emotions; fortunately, his intuition sees the ultimate value of this work.

Matt is thirty-five years old, good looking, and has a steady job. His girlfriend left him a year ago and he still misses her. He is afraid of confrontation and rejection. He imagines all the negative things that may happen and does not want risk being rejected. Many people who are highly intellectual and not in touch with their emotions suffer from loneliness, helplessness, and fear.

Matt constantly reads new books and listens to many spiritual teachers, yet nothing seems to help him face his fears. I suggested to Matt an exercise where he would approach a woman of any age to engage in small talk. The setting I suggested was in a grocery store, especially in the produce section.

I hope that as he learns to get in touch with his feelings and emotions, he can surrender to them through the process of journaling and factualizing the events that trigger him. With time and effort, this process will stimulate his intuitive intelligence, the awakened thinking mind.

We must learn how to differentiate between our ego-intellect, which depends on memory and lives in the past, and the awakened mind. The idea is to awaken the mind that lives in the reality of the now, loves to factualize when our feelings and emotions are triggered, and loves to work on problems in order to understand.

Idea of Effort

Everyone applies different levels of effort to their job, exercise, communication, education, and in relationships. Some put in a great effort in certain areas and low efforts in others.

I want to emphasize that we do not have free will and instead follow the law of necessity. This means that we follow from our conditioned nature, the knowledge acquired, and what is stored in our memory.

Many years ago, when I first met my teacher, he thought that I would not be a good candidate for his work which required mental thinking. Unfortunately, at that time I felt mentally weak, and I lived from my emotions. However, through years of effort applying reason and intuition I realized that I could think, and my mind began to strengthen itself with prolonged effort.

Over the years I wondered why students who were exposed to a teacher's great wisdom would leave the group. Later it became clearer to me that people leave because it is all about desire, motivation, what they genuinely want, and how much effort are they willing to invest.

It takes great effort to understand Spinoza and Gurdjieff's teachings and it is my greatest joy to share Spinoza's clarity and truth with as many people possible.

Ben Case Study

Ben is called the fix-it man who solves all of his family and friends' problems. Growing up, he was the middle child of seven siblings, and everyone would go to Ben to complain about the others.

Ben has a naturally positive and calming demeanor. He always wants to stop the pain others feel by listening and helping to solve their problems. I mentioned to Ben that on his tombstone the inscription may read, "He gave his life to others and lost his own in the process."

This had a deep effect on him. Ben also realized that the idea he must learn to understand is that his wanting to stop the pain in his children was preventing them from learning and therefore depriving them of growth. Pain is an indication that we feel powerless and helpless because the problems we are facing require more effort to understand and solve.

Ben has taken this work deeply and seriously and it has benefited him greatly. He has made great progress and is coming to a new sense of self, a new reality, and new direction for his life. So much so that his ex-wife Jennifer saw the positive changes in his character and decided to join our group. Likewise, his son Jason was so affected by these changes in his dad that he too decided to participate in our study group.

Jennifer Case Study

Jennifer has been with me for two months and is making great progress in such a short time. This is the advantage of working directly one on one with me. Yes, it is challenging; however, what took me ten years working with my teacher in a general group setting, it may take two years for my students to achieve the same working one on one with them.

Jennifer told me about an experience that upset her. She wanted to pick up a few groceries from a corner market that is close to home. She was in a hurry, but feared that a cashier named Cindy who loves to talk and ask a lot of questions would stop her and take too much of her time.

Jennifer did not want to appear rude and cut Cindy short. Jennifer likes Cindy and thinks the other woman is so sweet. Normally she loves talking to Cindy when she has time, but on that day Jennifer was in a hurry and did not want Cindy to feel insulted.

I suggested to Jennifer that she journal about the feelings and emotions which had been triggered. She felt stress, anxiety, pain, hate, and anger. Feelings of stress and anxiety indicate that our desires are not being met.

The specific emotions are a) desire, when we want something, and then b) pain arises when our desires are not met.

Jennifer imagined Cindy as the cause of her pain. This resulted in the emotion of hate. Hate is pain connected with the idea that Cindy is the cause. What follows hate is anger. Anger is desire through hatred where we want to remove or destroy the cause of our pain.

What we need to understand is that every day we are affected in many ways by external events and circumstances. Growth is a process of journaling and acknowledging that we are in a state of confusion.

As we begin to see that when our desires are not met, we really do not know what to do at that moment. Feelings of powerlessness, helplessness, and confusion manifest. Anger is a way of dealing with our problems.

In Jennifer's case, she avoids the problem by not going to the market unless she's in the mood to chat. She is enjoying the process of understanding through journaling. By writing down her thoughts, experiences, feelings, and emotions that were triggered, this activity is beginning to make her feel more calm and powerful.

The more she does this the more her sense of self develops, and a deeper self-awareness begins to appear. Jennifer is getting in touch with a higher active part of her mind. This is the understanding, and it requires exercise by facing problems that seem overwhelming to the passive state of mind.

A Final Note

Now that you have gone through this book, it may have seemed difficult. Maybe not. You might have related to it, or not at all. However, what's important is that you may have gained something within yourself just by reading it.

A feeling that says, "I can do this. I feel more insightful. I understand how to factualize and apply myself with more effort in whatever I do."

This is what I wanted to communicate in this book, that we all have a higher level of intelligence, a more conscious and aware state of being. Maybe you are ready to study the books I recommended. If not, that's okay.

Just remember that you are an intelligent spiritual being, and that inwardly you need to be fed with material that complements your nature, and no matter what you choose, you will do yourself a favor.

Bye for now. God Bless.

BIBLIOGRAPHY

Grover, Gregory, *How to Solve Life's Problems*, Almeida Publications, 2014

Kettner, Frederick, *Back to the Nameless One*, Lewis Almeida, 2021

Maté, Gabor, M.D., *When the Body Says No*, John Wiley & Sons, Inc., 2003

Ouspensky, P.D., *In Search of the Miraculous*, Harcourt Brace & Company, 1949

Spinoza, Benedict de, *The Ethics*, Translated by R.H.M. Elwes, Dover Publications, New York, 1955

Tsabary, Shefali, Ph.D., *The Conscious Parent*, Namaste Publishing, 2010

ABOUT THE AUTHOR

Lewis Almeida is a Mexican American born in 1941. He comes from a large family of ten siblings and grew up relatively poor on a four-acre parcel in Torrance, California. His father was self-employed.

Lewis became a hair stylist at the age of twenty-two and moved to the small community of Corona, where he married and eventually started his own hair salon. Years later after his divorce, he moved to Santa Monica to be closer to his mentor and teacher, the late Gregory Grover.

Mr. Grover introduced Lewis to the works of Gurdjieff and Spinoza, whose philosophical teachings changed his character and the direction of his life. For over forty-five years, Almeida has dedicated his life to this important work.

Lewis declares, "I will always be grateful to Gregory Grover because he encouraged me to put in more effort developing my feelings and bringing them to clear ideas. I know who I am. I am a happy man with a purpose and a deep meaning in my life."

His website is WayofSpinoza.com.

Printed in Great Britain
by Amazon